Around

with

The Ramblers

30 Circular Walks

**between four and ten miles
devised by local Ramblers**

compiled and edited by Sheila Smith

ISBN 978-1-906494-19-3

Introduction

The walks in this book have been previously published in the monthly magazine EDP Norfolk and they have now been collected together to make them available for more walkers. When from 2001 our walks were first published in the Magazine, they were coordinated and usually written by Allan Jones, with maps drawn by Ian Smith, both members of Ramblers' King's Lynn Group. In 2006 they decided that five years was long enough and I took over the task on a temporary basis - but finding I did enjoy the job, I am still doing it in 2010.

The shortest walk is just four miles and the longest is ten miles. However, the longer walks include shorter options, so they should all be within the capacity of regular walkers of all ages. Some of the walks overlap to a small extent and may be combined to create longer routes for more ambitious walkers (9+11, 11+16, 13+14, 18+24, and 21+25). The presentation of this book is more elaborate than for any of our previous publications, but one thing stays the same - each walk is complete within a two page spread. The scale of the maps varies, some are constricted by the width of the page, but others are larger, using the available space.

Since 2006 I have had help from many Rambler members, not least Allan Jones, though none of his walks appear here as he is preparing his own book (which is why there are few walks for the west of the county in this one). Help from other members is shown on the contents page.   I am particularly grateful to members who accompanied me while reconnoitring the walks. These include Sheila Freake, Margaret Pearce and Margaret Wilde, but especially Barbara Ives who came with me on numerous occasions, often providing transport as well. Sue Walker provided encouragement and advice, and lastly (in sequence of events) Diana de Jager did the proof reading, making considerable improvements.

Photographs were supplied by Sue Walker walk 3, Roland Smith walk 6, Janet Stevens (picture of the Bure) walk 15, Sheringham Group member walk 22, Tim Rushton walk 30. The remainder are my own and I drew the maps, with some variations in presentation, the earlier ones being more basic. With practice they evolved, enabling more detail to be included. There has been some editing for essential adjustments and to introduce minimal standardisation, but substantial re-drawing was not feasible in the time available.

Sheila Smith - Editor

February 2010

Contents

We are grateful to all the individuals named above who provided walks, some used basically as supplied, while others were edited or adapted for varying reasons. The remaining walks were all devised by the editor, but with thanks to Gillian Kent for help and advice on Walk 8.

See walk headings for relevant Ordnance Survey maps, Landranger (L) or Explorer (E).

1 Colton and Barford - Four miles. OS - L 144, E 237, Ref 105093

This walk starts at the car park on the east side of Colton Church. It is easy walking through varied countryside with field and woodland paths as well as some quiet roads and a short stretch across Barnham Broom Golf Course. The route crosses the river Yare twice, not far from its source. Look out for wild flowers.

1 From the car park turn right along the road. Just beyond Church House and a footpath on the right, turn left over a footbridge and continue along a field edge. At a field corner go through to the right and then bear left following a hedged green path. Keep to the right and ignore a path through the trees, turn right along the road. On the left you will soon see a splendid brick barn with stepped gables, each

The pond

step capped with a ridge tile. It bears the date 1666 and initials "IM" formed in the brickwork. Soon on the right there is an attractive pond and then the village sign. Turn left at a staggered cross roads and after a further 200 yards fork right on a track besides a clump of trees. When the track reaches the woods it turns to the right. Follow the track into a clearing in the woods, which are awash with bluebells in the spring.

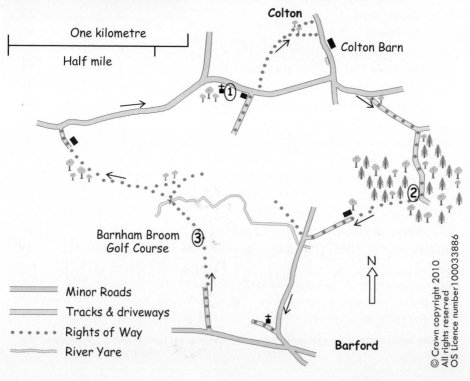

One kilometre

Half mile

Colton

Colton Barn

①

②

Barnham Broom
Golf Course ③

N

Minor Roads

Tracks & driveways

Rights of Way

River Yare

Barford

Colton Barn

2 When the track widens and goes leftwards turn right on a marked path through the trees. At the end of the woods the path briefly turns left, then right. Continue beyond a farm along a track with a line of poplars. At the end of the track go through the gate on the right and turn left along the road, soon crossing the infant Yare. Continue to Barford Church, along a short track to the right, just before the cross roads. St. Botolph's dates from the 12th or 13th century and much of the architecture is Early English and Perpendicular. Any group who would like to visit the church are invited to phone beforehand (01603 759426) to arrange for it to be open. Return to the road and continue to the junction and turn right. This road can be quite busy with fast traffic, take care. After a quarter mile turn right along a track with a hedge on the left. On reaching the golf course bear to the right around the edge of an old gate onto a hedged path alongside the edge of the course.

3 Follow a waymarked path to the left over the golf course, keeping alert for Golfers. Go across a footbridge over the Yare and initially bear right, but at the top of the bank bear to the left making for a waymark at the opposite corner of the field. Continue ahead with the golf course on the left, follow a sign through a gap on the right, then left along a field edge. Follow around the edge of a field to go through a gap on the left, go ahead to a stile and follow the marked path across a garden, out through a gate and then follow the driveway, turn right along the road and back to the church. St. Andrew's Colton also dates from the 13th century, but has been much restored. There is a rare 14th century wall painting inside, depicting two women indulging in the dreadful sin of gossip and being encouraged by devils! It can be viewed from the Victorian Gothic organ gallery.

Colton Church

2 Banham – Four and a half miles.   OS - L 144, E 230, Ref 064882

This walk starts from the village green in front of the church in Banham, where there is space to park by the edges of the green. Banham has been a settlement since at least Saxon times and has several entries in the Domesday Book including mention of three manors. St. Mary's Church dates mainly from the 14th century with a Victorian restoration. It has an impressive spire, splendid beamed roof with kingposts and queenposts and good stained glass. There is a 14th century wooden effigy of a knight, said to represent the founder Sir Hugh Bardolph, but as he died

The Guildhall

in 1203 this is probably somewhat fanciful, and presumably the present church replaced a 12th century structure. The small green is quite delightful, with village sign, war memorial, and a few trees, all within a square comprising the church and fine old houses. The timber framed houses on the north side were originally the Guildhall, also serving as a manor court and a jail.

1 Facing the church, turn right to take the track, known as The Spong, running to the left of the timber framed houses. Spong means a wet muddy place, but fortunately this does not seem to be an appropriate description now for this lane. Turn left at a T junction onto a footpath – soon there are good views of the church spire on the left. Turn right along Backslough Lane and left along Greyhound Road. Go over the cross roads by the Garden House PH; both this and the PH near Banham Zoo were originally cider pubs (no beer), a reflection of the long tradition of cider making in the village. Gaymers produced "cyder" at their farm in Banham for much of the 19th century until they moved their operations to larger premises in Attleborough in 1896. Now that site too has been transferred to other uses and Gaymers no longer operate in Norfolk. However cider is still produced on a small scale in Banham. After about 120 yards, turn left on a footpath to follow field edges left and right around the back of a garden, then continue ahead. At a very narrow field the right of way crosses diagonally, but many choose to keep to the edge then turn right at the cor-ner and then left rejoining the right of way. Continue along the field edges for nearly a mile to New Lane and turn left down the hill then right at the T junction.

The Church from the south

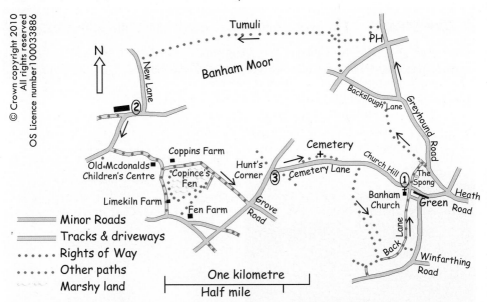

2 Continue around the bend, ignoring a track to the right, then turn left along the driveway to Old Macdonald's Children's Centre. Continue past the car park and turn right around the timber clad building, then very soon left along a track past Coppins Farm. The possibility of using the footpath around the edges of Copince's Fen was investigated, but at the time of writing there was a lack of footbridges, both on this and the more southerly path close to where they join. They are shown on the map, as some walkers may care to investigate in hope of improvement. In drier conditions, or for the long legged and agile, they may be passable anyway. Otherwise follow the track round a corner and continue to a road. Cross to the far side of the road and turn left along it (this road can be quite busy, take care).

3 Turn right at Hunt's Corner into Cemetery Lane. Near this corner is the site of a 19th century brickworks. Just beyond the houses turn left into the cemetery, used as an extension to the churchyard, and continue past the rather forlorn ruined chapel and out via the gateway at the far end. Continue along the road, now Church Hill, then turn right through a metal kissing gate, bear slightly right across the meadow to keep a large tree on your left, then follow the hedge on the right. Once again there are good views of the church to the left. At a corner where the right of way should continue ahead, go a little to the left and through rails by a gate to follow a permissive alternative. Follow a left edge to another corner, turn right then left to rejoin the right of way. At the end of this field turn left along Back Lane; at first little more than a path, it soon becomes a narrow track. Continue back to the church passing behind the school, the community centre and a 14th century house restored by the Norfolk Historic Buildings Trust and reputed to be one of the oldest dwellings in Norfolk.

3 Overstrand – Four and a half miles.   OS - L 133, E 252, Ref 247411

Start from the Public Car Park in Overstrand (there is a charge). The walk has many varied landscapes; cliff top views, open countryside, a beautiful churchyard, an "International Airport", a Hungry Hill and a Shrieking Pit! The walk could be very satisfactorily finished off with a visit to the Cliff Top Cafe.

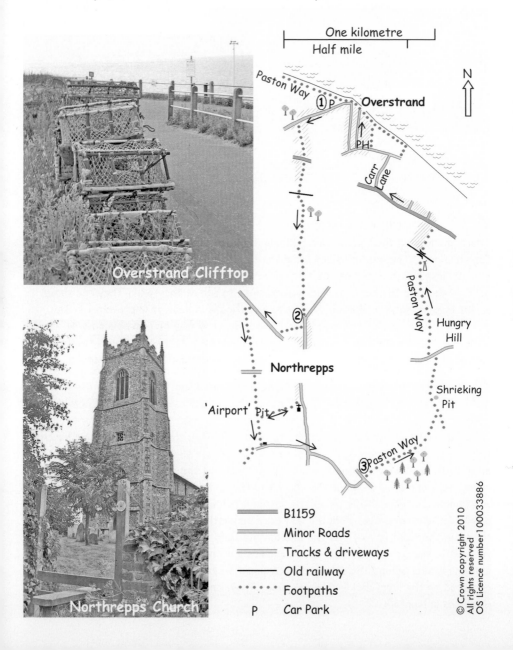

Overstrand Clifftop

Northrepps Church

One kilometre
Half mile

N

Paston Way
① P Overstrand
PH
Carr Lane
Paston Way
Hungry Hill
Shrieking Pit
②
Northrepps
'Airport' Pit
③ Paston Way

B1159
Minor Roads
Tracks & driveways
Old railway
Footpaths
P   Car Park

1 Turn right out of the car park, and continue walking inland along the road, passing the entrance to The Close. A few yards further on the left is the entrance to the first footpath. Turn into it and follow it to its end, cross the usually busy coast road and take the next footpath straight up the hill. This takes you across the route of a disused railway line, continues up through some trees, and at the top opens out to a glorious inland view. The village of Northrepps is there before you, complete with its church. After taking in the view, follow the path as it goes down-hill with a hedge on the left, towards the village and a road.

2 At the road turn right for about 100 yards, passing some interesting little cottages, before turning right onto another footpath. Soon there is another road, turn right and continue for about 250 yards, and at a hedgerow on the left, turn left onto a track, then immediately left again onto a field edge path, with the hedge on your right. Cross the next road, and look to your right down the road, and there you can see the building and wind-sock of the "International Airport" at Northrepps! It was closed at the time we walked by. Follow the path, which becomes very narrow and is often wet, but after passing a disused pit, it opens out again, with a footpath on the left going to St. Mary's church (mainly Perpendicular, but with earlier remnants). The churchyard can be accessed from the path, it is beautifully kept and is worth taking a detour at any time. After visiting the church, carry on in a southerly direction down to the cottages and a track. Go left along the track with the cottages on your left to a road, first turn right, then left at a road junction with a rough pasture in the field on your left. Here there was a barn owl hunting, and we had several splendid views of him. At the next junction keep left - this is where the walk joins the route of the Paston Way as it goes to Overstrand. Carry on along the road a short way to a T-junction, where the Paston Way goes across the road and enters a footpath through a way-marked entrance.

3 The path leads up through a wood and on to a track by a wood on the right. At the end of the wood, the track goes left, and is soon joined by another track from the right. Keep left at this junction and follow the track past the Shrieking Pit - a copy of the legend of the pit was pinned on a tree on the banks of the pit to the right. Continue along the track to a road to Hungry Hill. Turn left along the road and soon right along the Paston Way again, which will lead you past a mast on the right and then into a wood and under a railway bridge. Carry on through the wood to the coastal road again. Cross and turn left and walk along the pavement for about a third of a mile. Turn right into Carr Lane, following the marker for the Paston Way. Go past a caravan park, take the road to the left past the Sea Marge Hotel and turn right immediately after the White Horse public house. At the Cliff Top Café turn left and walk along the cliff top back to the car park.

Overstrand Coastline

4 Hapton, Toprow & Flordon - Four and three-quarter miles.
OS - L 134+144, E 237, Ref 176967

This walk starts at St. Margaret's Church Hapton, There is limited parking outside the church when no service is in progress. The church was much restored 160 years ago, the tower is wholly Victorian, but the origins of the church are much older – at least 13th century. Close to the church, Meeting House Field, with a table and benches, could be a good place for a picnic at the end of the walk.

1 With the church behind you, turn left along the road then go straight ahead along the track from the corner. Just before a hedged boundary on your left, turn

right on a green field path. Go left at the next field corner then follow the path as it turns right. At a T junction go left and follow the track as it bends to the right by a bungalow and out to the road. Turn left - you may soon note the line of an old railway embankment crossing the road then disappearing where it once crossed the field on the left. Follow the road sharply round to the right where it becomes Blacksmiths

Hapton Church

Lane instead of High Road and pass St. Mary's Chapel and Chantry House on the left. Turn right along a track under the old railway line, just as the embankment reappears. Keep to the left at a junction with driveways – note the interesting roofscapes in Toprow, then turn right along the village street.

2 Immediately before a bend and a white gate leading to some large sheds, turn left through the edge of a field and into a clear tree lined track. Beyond the track the route continues along a field edge, go over a footbridge and diagonally across a field bearing slightly to the right and over another footbridge, then up a slope following a path passing old sand and gravel workings on the left. Turn right along a road, then just before white railings on the edge of a bridge, go over a stile to the left into Flordon Common, an S.S.S.I. In June you may expect to find a beautiful assortment of wild flowers, including flag iris and other damp loving varieties. If you choose to try this walk in the winter or after any prolonged period of rain you may find conditions very soggy underfoot. Follow the path over foot-bridges and into an open field, across a playing field to another footbridge leading into a play area. The exit to the road in Flordon is just to the right of the children's play equipment.

3 Turn right along the road, ignoring a road on the left. You may visit St. Michael's Church which is well hidden along a narrow path to the left. It has Saxon windows and other parts have been added and altered throughout the centuries. Until 1774 there was a round tower, now replaced with a brick wall and a Victorian bellcote. It is generally open on Saturdays between 10 am and 4 pm and the key is available locally at other times. Beyond the church the route soon turns right across a bridge over the stream into the Hapton Estate, following the Tas Valley Way. The estate is one of the centres for the Redwings Horse Sanctuary and you will see

rescued horses, ponies and donkeys in the well-fenced fields beside the path; due to their past experiences some of them may be rather nervous and it is advisable not to approach them. When reaching the stables the path turns to the right before the last two buildings, going through a yard, then bears left before going right along a drive-way with a sign saying "no exit before 4 pm". At a point where the driveway bends a little to the right the footpath goes to the left following round a fenced field edge. Turn sharp right along a minor road, Cow Lane, and follow it back to Holly Lane and Hapton Church.

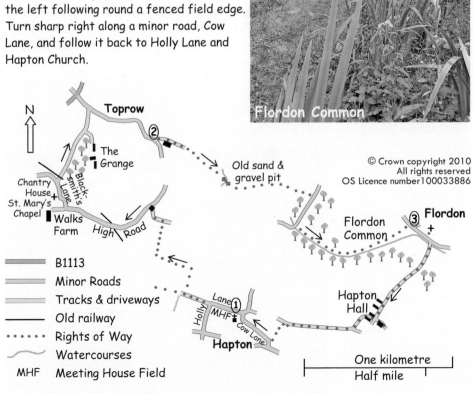

Flordon Common

© Crown copyright 2010
All rights reserved
OS Licence number 100033886

Legend:

- ═══ B1113
- ═══ Minor Roads
- ═══ Tracks & driveways
- ── Old railway
- ••••• Rights of Way
- ∿ Watercourses
- MHF Meeting House Field

One kilometre

Half mile

5 Knapton & Paston - Five miles.   OS - L 143, E 252, Ref 301331

The Paston Way which links North Walsham and Cromer is noted for visiting 15 churches and 15 towns and villages on its twenty mile route. This walk includes part of the Way in the parishes of Knapton and Paston, but does not pass through any village or visit any church – although a short diversion to visit Knapton and its church will add just half a mile to the route. It does include attractive hedged green lanes, wider views, an old canal and a nature reserve in an old railway cutting. Start at the car park on the western side of Old Hall Street south of Knapton where the old railway crosses the road (look for the car park, the railway is easy to miss at this point). You may choose to approach via minor roads from either B1145 or B1150. There is alternative parking at the north east corner of Pigney's Wood – you could adapt the walk to start from there.

1 From the car park cross the road and take the narrow fenced path opposite. At the end of the fencing go right to follow the path across two fields. Go through a gap in the hedge and turn left with the Paston Way. A low lying section of the track is subject to flooding; if you do meet this problem find a gap in the hedge on your left and follow along the edge until a field track provides access back to the main track. On reaching a junction of tracks, with a minor road ahead and a big house on your left, you may turn left to visit Knapton (and return by the same route) otherwise turn right on a path across two fields. Turn right along a road and pass a junction on the left, where we diverge from the Paston Way.

2 After another 100 yards the road bears right, but go ahead onto a narrow track. Continue along this, ignoring paths to left and right, to reach a junction with another track and a road by Barcham's Farmhouse.   Turn right along the road,

continue over a cross roads then after another 100 yards turn left on a cross field path. Continue ahead with a field boundary on the right and at the end of this go a few yards to the right, through into the next field and turn left along a left edge through to a minor road and turn left. Turn right along B1150 for about 50 yards.

Knapton Cutting in winter

3 Turn right along a footpath by the disused North Walsham and Dilham Canal. This canalisation of the River Ant, between Swafield Bridge and Smallburgh, was just eight and three quarter miles long, first surveyed in 1811, authorised by Act of Parliament in 1812 and cut in 1825/26. The only canal in Norfolk with locks, it was built wider than standard to accommodate wherries. It cost £30,000 to build, but when it was sold in 1885 it realised only £600 – which would have been bad enough, but the company's solicitor absconded with the proceeds! Never very profitable, it closed for commercial traffic in 1935. There are recent proposals for restoration, but currently parts of the canal are overgrown and silted up. This area is very marshy - fortunately, however, the path is raised and firm. Keep along this path following the line of the canal until you can go no further, then turn right over a footbridge. Follow this path alongside the edge of Pigney's Wood, a community woodland, to a junction by a flint barn with seats and picnic tables, plus information about birds, butterflies, mammals of Britain, wild flowers, garden insects, wild fruits and berries and fungi. From the barn turn half left, ignore paths going uphill, go ahead through a field with woodland on either side to meet an embankment. Bear right then up the steps onto the Paston Way running along the course of the old rail-way line, firstly along the embankment, then through Knapton Cutting, a butterfly nature reserve. It is beautiful in winter, in spring or summer it will be very special indeed. Keep to the railway passing beneath a minor road then after another quarter of a mile go up a long flight of steps back to the car park.

Information about the Paston Way is available from Norfolk County Council 01603 223317 or www.countrysideaccess.norfolk.gov.uk

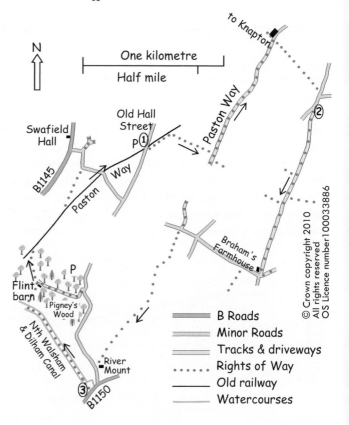

	B Roads
	Minor Roads
	Tracks & driveways
	Rights of Way
	Old railway
	Watercourses

6 Reepham - 5 miles.   OS - L 133, E 238, Ref 098234

This walk goes around Reepham, but hardly touches the town, although it is well worth
a visit. The route ends with a short section along Marriott's Way, a recreational route
along old railway lines between Norwich and Aylsham. The first section of this walk
uses the "Themelthorpe Link Path" for the Way, providing a short cut to avoid the full
loop of the Way via the Themelthorpe Curve. The 180 degree Curve was constructed
in 1960,connecting what remained of the lines after partial closures and was then the
sharpest bend in the British Rail Network. However the Curve and the remainder of
the line were closed in 1985 when concrete production ceased at Lenwade. Marriott's
Way is named after William Marriott (1857-1943). He was employed initially by the
Eastern & Midlands Railway and then, following a merger in 1893, by the Midland &
Great Northern. He was Engineer from 1883, Locomotive Superintendent from 1885

and Traffic Manager from 1919 and he continued in all the posts until his retirement in 1924. He was an innovative and talented engineer, a pioneer of reinforced concrete and he made many improvements to track design. It is good that his life and achievements are commemorated, but no doubt he would have expected and wished that the railways should continue in use. The idea of a "recreational path" would have been a quite alien concept!

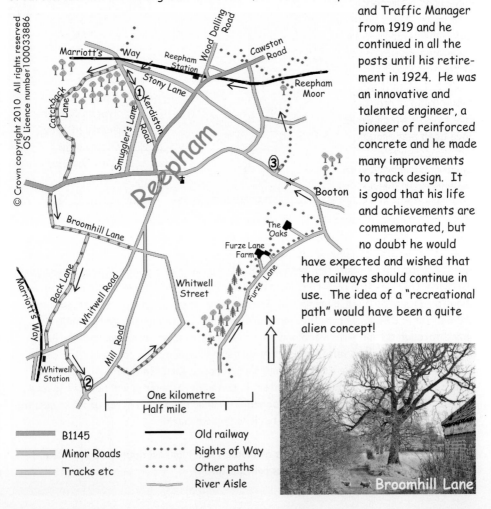

Broomhill Lane

Most of this walk is on good tracks and minor roads, but be prepared for one fairly short path which may be very wet. Start from the car park on the east side of Kerdiston Road on the north-west edge of Reepham.

1 Turn right along the road then just before the railway bridge turn left along Catchback Lane. Carefully cross the B1145, so you can see (and be seen) around the bend, turn right and soon left along a rough tarmac track, Broomhill Lane. At the second house the track goes round to the left and becomes a green lane. Turn right on Back Lane between a hedge and a wire fence. The track meets Whitwell Road by the side of Marriott's Way. As an optional diversion, join the Way and cross the road via the bridge to visit Whitwell Station – a railway preservation society is planning restoration projects. Return over the bridge then down to the road, turn left and at the top of the hill go right along a track, keeping left by a hedge.

2 Turn left along Mill Road, then immediately before a barn turn right along a hedged path. At a corner, and a junction with a signed Stewardship path (access officially ceased in 2002 but it is apparently still open), turn left with the path, which widens to become more like a track and then a narrow road. When the road is approaching Whitwell Street and bends sharply to the left, turn right over a stile to a footpath. This is the path which might be rather wet, firstly over marshy ground and then after crossing a footbridge. Go straight ahead, ignoring a path going diagonally left. Turn left along a Furze Lane. There are DEFRA Stewardship Walks on the left hand side of the lane, providing an option to walk along field edges. There is access at the most southerly point (as shown on the map) and adjacent to the farm driveways, but no access or egress at the road junction at the far end. Turn left at the T junction along a rather busy road. Ignore the turning to the right and follow the road round to the left, past cottages in Booton and over the river.

3 Turn right on a track with a locked wire gate, but a stile on the left and a gap on the right. Beyond a large shed the track becomes a field path. Near the end of the field the path bears to the left over a stile and a footbridge then bears round to the right, through a kissing gate, then follows a fenced green track between gardens and out to a road. Turn left, then in a few yards turn right, beside a lovely old house, along a field edge path. Shortly before the path reaches Marriotts Way the track turns sharply left through the trees, then joins Marriotts Way. Turn left and continue to Cawston Road, go left then soon right into Wood Dalling Road and left under the railway bridge back onto Marriott's Way. Pass the old Reepham Station, where there is a tea shop and small museum. Before reaching the bridge over Kerdiston Road turn left on a short link path to Stony Lane, turn right then left onto Kerdiston Road and back to the car park.

A leaflet about the Marriott's Way is available from Norfolk County Council (phone 01603 222769)

7 Swannington Upgate - Five miles.   OS - L 133, E 238, Ref 142183

This walk is a variation of the Wynch's Way, a waymarked local route named for the family who lived at Swannington Manor until the late twentieth century. Start from the western end of the Common at Swannington Upgate where there is limited parking.

1 Cross the road to a grassy path passing in front of Corner Cottage. The route follows Wynch's Way and heads in a south westerly direction. Cross the Reepham Road and continue straight ahead. Go gradually downhill then up the steps to join Marriott's Way along the old railway line. Marriott's Way, for walkers and cyclists, goes from Norwich to Aylsham, taking a loop around Reepham via Themwelthorpe and following the old railway all the way. Turn right towards Reepham, then, beyond the track going diagonally beneath the railway, turn right on a track through a gap in the hedge. Follow the field edge track initially parallel to Marriott's Way, but then just before reaching the road turn right again uphill beside a belt of pines. Emerge on Station Road near some white houses.

2 Turn right and just after reaching wooded Alderford Common take a well defined path on your left. Initially this runs close to the edge of the common, but after descending some steps down into an old marl pit, it strikes to the right across the middle. The pit was dug about 100 years ago when the Lord of the Manor rented out the mineral rights to local farmers and the marl was spread on nearby fields to improve fertility. They reached the underlying chalk, now resulting in chalk grassland, rare in this part of Norfolk. The chalk underlying most of Norfolk slopes downwards to the east and is more likely to outcrop in the west of the county. Alderford Common is noted for wild flowers favoured by the chalk, migrant song birds, particularly nightingales, and crested newts in the ponds. There is also a Bronze Age burial mound nearby. At a small car park re-cross the Reepham Road and continue on a footpath opposite. The OS map shows the definitive route diagonally across the field, but the waymarked route is shown following the left hand boundary and turning right at the field corner. After passing Lower Farm the path goes through a gap in the hedge on the left to join the farm drive and continues to Broad Lane. Turn left and left again through Swannington village passing the village pump with its thatched canopy on the green and the entrance to the Manor and the Romantic Gardens Nursery.

Swannington Village Pump

3 At St. Margaret's Church and the Old Rectory turn right into Church Lane. Much of the church dates from the 13th century and the porch is 15th century. Just after Swannington Hall, a grand Elizabethan house with a moat, leave the lane and go straight ahead onto the grassy footpath going steadily uphill. Turn right on a crossing track to The Woodlands. At the farm buildings turn right, then almost immediately left, pass the farmhouse and another house. Then turn sharply left through a farm gate to follow a field edge path, then diagonally right on a clear path

Upgate Common

across a field corner, meeting the corner of Swiffer's Lane (or Swift Foot Lane), reputedly used by smugglers. Bear right on the track going south to Upgate Common. Cross a wooden bridge and then turn right to follow a board-walk, initially beside a stream. Swannington Brook is the least polluted of the Wensum tributaries, trout thrive, and the nearby ponds attract toads to migrate up to three miles to lay their eggs. Follow the path uphill then join a track returning to the start.

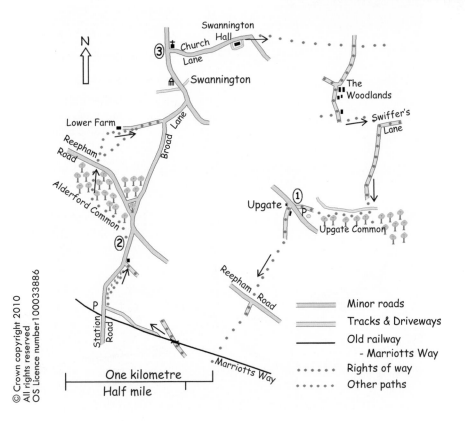

Minor roads		
Tracks & Driveways		
Old railway - Marriotts Way		
Rights of way		
Other paths		

One kilometre
Half mile

8 Bengate and Weavers' Way – Five and a quarter miles.

OS - L 133, E 252/OL40, Ref 306274

This walk starts at Bengate on the Weavers' Way, about two and a half miles south-east of North Walsham. There is a small car park just south of the A149. The beginning of the walk, over fields with wide views across undulating countryside, contrasts with the last section along an old railway track, now reminiscent of a sheltered woodland trail. This was once part of the Midland and Great Northern line (locally known as "Muddle and Go Nowhere"), carrying many passengers, including at different times, holiday makers, troops, school children and evacuees. Freight included locally grown produce and fish from Yarmouth.

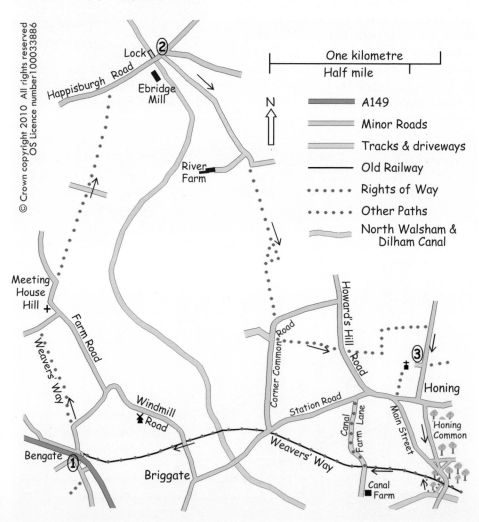

1 From the car park go under the main road via the old railway bridge, turn left, then when the track reaches the road turn sharp right on a minor road. As this bends to the right bear left through a gap to go ahead on a footpath. Continue ahead through kissing gates and out to a road, turn right then left at a junction. When the road bends to the left leave the Weavers' Way, turn right on a footpath and continue straight ahead, passing

View across the fields

a wartime pillbox at the highest point. Turn right along Happisburgh Road, take care as it can be quite busy. Cross the canal and note the old lock on the left.

Honing Church

2 Immediately beyond the canal turn right along a broad gravel track towards River Farm. Pass the driveway to the farm then go ahead along a signed footpath. Where the right of way goes diagonally across a corner it may be easier continuing to the corner and going right and then left through a gap by a finger post. Continue to Corner Common Road and ahead for a short distance then left along a signed path. Cross Howard's Hill Road towards Honing Church, situated on raised ground with a tall Perpendicular tower. Follow the path to the left and right, then right along the road to the church, St Peter and St Paul.

3 Continue down the road to a junction, turn left and soon right, follow the road over Honing Common then continue to the bottom of two small greens. The right hand one has a wooden seat round a tree. On the right hand side of this green, over another road, there is a narrow footpath through the trees to the Weavers Way. Go across it, then almost immediately turn right on a permissive path to the old Honing Staithe at the end of a cut from the canal. When the canal was in operation this was a very busy place, bringing in supplies for the locality, including bricks from the Dilham brickworks. Outward goods included apples and locally made baskets. Go across the head of the staithe then go left to follow the cut down to the canal, then right along the canal towpath. Follow this almost to the edge of the woodland, then turn right over a dyke and back to the Weavers Way and turn left. Cross Canal Farm Lane and Station Road and pass the former Honing Station, then cross a grassy field with a seat, a pleasant place for a picnic, and go over Briggate Bridge. Around this area the North Walsham & Dilham Canal Trust are organising work parties to clear around the locks and the old mill to the south. Cross Windmill Road and along the final stretch, turn left and go under the main road to return to the car park.

9 Thorpe Abbotts and Billingford - Five and a quarter miles.
OS - L 156, E 230, Ref 177789

This walk starts and finishes on the Angles Way, the 78 mile long distance path between Great Yarmouth and Knettishall Heath. Start in the old piece of road south of the A143, opposite Kiln Lane; there is space for several cars, but keep the eastern end clear. It would be possible to reach this walk by bus - the 580 between Beccles and Diss runs along the A143 approximately hourly in both directions for much of the day (except Sunday) - in which case start the circuit at section 2. Walk 11 could be combined with this one to make a route of just over nine miles. They overlap by about three-quarters of a mile and this length would be omitted.

1 Turn south onto a track following the Angles Way almost to the river, turn left over a footbridge and continue along a field edge, the river just visible on the right. Ignore a stile and turn left keeping to the Angles Way, soon crossing a foot-bridge over a watercourse. This footbridge, installed late in 2008, was funded by the Southern Norfolk Group of the Ramblers' Association. Water levels here can be very variable, the former bridge was too low and liable to float away. Go ahead along a right edge. At a crossing track leave the Angles Way, our route goes ahead along a deep tree lined path, with good views of Thorpe Abbotts Church on the left. All Saints has Saxon origins, but the round tower is 13th century. For a closer look it would be easiest to do so after the walk; there is space to park. Although usually locked it may be possible to arrange access via the excellent website - www.allsaintsthorpeabbotts.com. Emerge onto the main road by a bus shelter.

2 Cross the A143, turn briefly right, then left towards Thorpe Abbotts, then immediately left again into a cut-off piece of road. Turn right onto a field edge footpath, continue ahead to a track, go left, keeping ahead when it becomes a field edge path, turn right along a good track, marked as permissive. Turn left opposite a pond by Wood Cottage following a track around a right edge. Near a communications mast bear left onto a grassy track to a field path with a belt of pines on the left.

Billingford Church

At the end of the pines turn right along the field edge. Just before a wood turn left over a footbridge, then right on a con-crete path (though the definitive route does go diagonally across the field). At the field corner go through to turn left on a good track. When the definitive route crosses diagonally, keep to the driveway turning right and left in front of Grove Farm.

3 At a road go ahead into Upper Street, initially a made up road, becoming a track beyond the houses. When the track turns left take a path to the right, continuing the former direction along a field edge. Beyond a narrow field the path should go diagonally right over a second narrow field, instead keep ahead along the field edge to turn right at the next field boundary. Just before Brick Kiln Farm, turn left over a footbridge, along a field edge beside a garden, then turn right (once again the definitive path is diagonal) then left along the driveway.

4 Just before the drive bends, turn left on a track alongside Brick Yard Plantation, continue on a good field edge path to a road. Go ahead along the road, turn left along a restricted byway, part of the Angles Way. Continue to Hall Farm, and then take a short diversion to the right to visit St Leonard's Church Billingford. This is shown on OS maps with no tower, but there is the base of one, rising just above the height of the nave – probably the building was never finished. The church, usually locked, has the key holder's phone number in the porch. Even without admission it is a delightful place to pause for a while, with a seat against the south wall and a fine view of the Waveney Valley and Billingford Windmill. Return to the crossing track and continue to Kiln Lane and turn right. Go straight across the A143 back to the start of the walk.

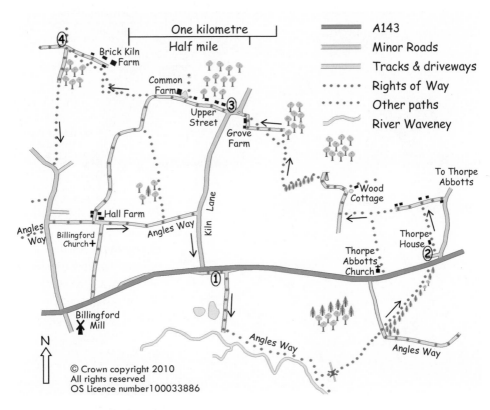

© Crown copyright 2010
All rights reserved
OS Licence number100033886

10 Rockland St. Mary – Five and a half miles with a shorter option.
OS - L 134, E OL40, Ref 328046

This walk uses part of the Wherryman's Way, the 35 mile recreational route from Norwich to Great Yarmouth, opened in 2005. It takes its name from the sailing barges and the men who provided transport for goods and people long before the railways and when most roads were merely rough tracks. We start at the Broads Authority Car Park by Rockland Staithe.

1 Turn left out of the car park, cross the head of the staithe and turn left along the Wherryman's Way. Continue past Rockland Broad, where you may wish to pause to take advantage of the bird hide, before following the path beside Short Dike, then the bank of the River Yare. Birds you may be fortunate enough to see around Rockland include mallard, tufted duck, common tern, greylag goose, Canada goose, heron, kingfisher and great crested grebe. The Broads were long thought to be a natural feature, but they are now known to be the result of medieval peat diggings. Just before the Beauchamp Arms leave the Wherryman's Way and turn right on a path leading away from the river. Continue past houses, out to a road.

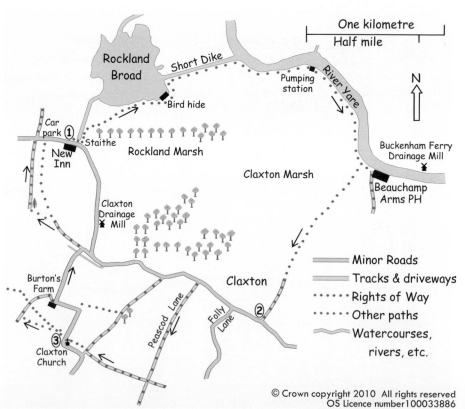

Rockland Broad and Short Dyke

Claxton Church

2 Turn right through Claxton and continue along the road past Folly Lane then, just beyond a barn conversion, turn left along Peascod Lane. *As an alternative, if you wish to shorten the walk, you may continue along the road, then go straight ahead when the main road turns sharp right and soon rejoin our route at the track from a bend.(*)* Follow the lane and bridleway for about half a mile – don't forget to pause to appreciate the views as the lane gently gains height – then, before reaching a line of pylons, turn right an a clear crossing track with Claxton Church ahead. At a T-junction turn right then almost immediately left, alongside a house, onto a path with a narrow entrance. Follow this path along a field edge, behind gardens, through into the churchyard. The nave of St. Andrews is Norman, and, although much altered and added to over the centuries, it retains the atmosphere of a simple country church - the underside of the thatch is visible in the roof. Go through the church gate to a road.

3 Cross the road to another path. The definitive line of the path cuts across the right hand corner, but it is easier to follow round the field edge, and then pass through a gap in the hedge. Again the definitive line should go ahead diagonally across the field, but there is a well-walked path along the field edge to your left, continuing on a clear track across an open field to a belt of trees ahead where you turn right on a crossing track. (Both paths are shown on the map, if you follow the definitive line turn right on the same crossing track). The track leads to a road by Burton's Farm, turn left and continue until, shortly after crossing a pretty stream, the road swings to the right. *(*)* Turn left away from the bend onto a track leading towards a house, The path on the OS map goes ahead across an open field, but the footpath in use goes to the left following around the boundary. Continue towards a small conifer wood, bearing left and right to join a clear track leading to the road at Rockland St. Mary. Once again both routes are shown on the map. Turn right and back to the start.

11 Brockdish and Thorpe Abbotts - Five and a half miles.
OS - L 156, E 230, Ref 204796

This walk starts from Brockdish Church, where there is limited parking when there are no services in progress. The older part of Brockdish village is further east, formerly the busy A143 ran along The Street, but it is now bypassed. It is an attractive village, with several houses dating from the 16th and 17th centuries, and a stream running alongside a minor road, and it still has a pub. Probably the medieval village centre was much closer to the church? Like walk 9 this route also uses part of the Angles Way and includes some ancient trackways. Neither the Angles Way nor this area of the Norfolk/Suffolk borders receive as much appreciation from walkers as they deserve; do try these walks for a taste of what they have to offer.

1 From the starting place in front of the church go back along the lane and turn right at the end and shortly left, just before houses, on a clear field edge path. Continue on this right edge then swing left across the field towards a copse, then right, and follow the path to the road – we now leave the Angles Way. Go left underneath the A143, then up the steps on the far side of a driveway on your right and turn right at the top. Follow the field edge, then as the path swings round to the north, near farm buildings, go right and immediately left onto a narrow hedged path then continue along field edges. At the end of the hedge turn left, then at a field corner follow the path around to the right.

2 Turn left along Whitepost Lane and at the corner continue ahead along Back Road. Shortly after passing a junction on your right turn left along Mormor Lane, a hedged track, and continue to its end. Go right to Thorpe Abbotts - you will pass Thorpe Abbotts Place on your left which is built on the site of the former manor house of Brockdish Earl. Pause to appreciate the village pump and well at the road junction; this was given to the parish in 1867, was restored in 1924 by a member of the original benefactor's family and in 1979 the canopy was restored by the people of the parish. From the pump take the road to the left, you will shortly pass the village sign on your right – this was unveiled in 1992 to commemorate the arrival of 100th Bomb Group USAAF in 1942. The memorial was a joint donation from the villagers and members of the 100th Bomb Group Association. (The site of the airfield is north-west of the village, you will easily identify it on the OS map, - there is a museum in the old control tower, open weekends and bank holidays during most of the year and Wednesdays in summer - however our route does not take us in that direction.) After about a further 400 yards turn right along School Lane by Pine Tree Cottage, then left, opposite Mill Pightle, along a field edge with a hedge on your left, go across a footbridge in the corner and continue ahead, now with the hedge on your right.

Memorial Sign

3 At the road junction cross the A143 to the left of the bus shelter and follow the narrow hedged path ahead. Across the field to the right you will have a view of Thorpe Abbotts All Saints Church standing beside the A143, even further from its village than Brockdish church. At a junction with a wider track turn left, to rejoin the Angles Way. The Waveney is to your right, beyond the water meadows, and higher land is to your left; clearly this track developed along the closest line to the river not subject to regular flooding. Keep with the track as it turns uphill to the A143 and immediately before it reaches the main road turn right onto a section of old cut-off road, although initially this appears to be just a footpath. Go round the side of a gate and join the road leading to Brockdish. In about 100 yards at the end of a hedge on your left, turn left onto a clear path. Follow the footpath to the right just before reaching the A143. Go right through the gate into a playing field and return to Brockdish church. The church is dedicated to St. Peter and St. Paul, and is mainly 14th century, but there are some Saxon and Norman remnants.

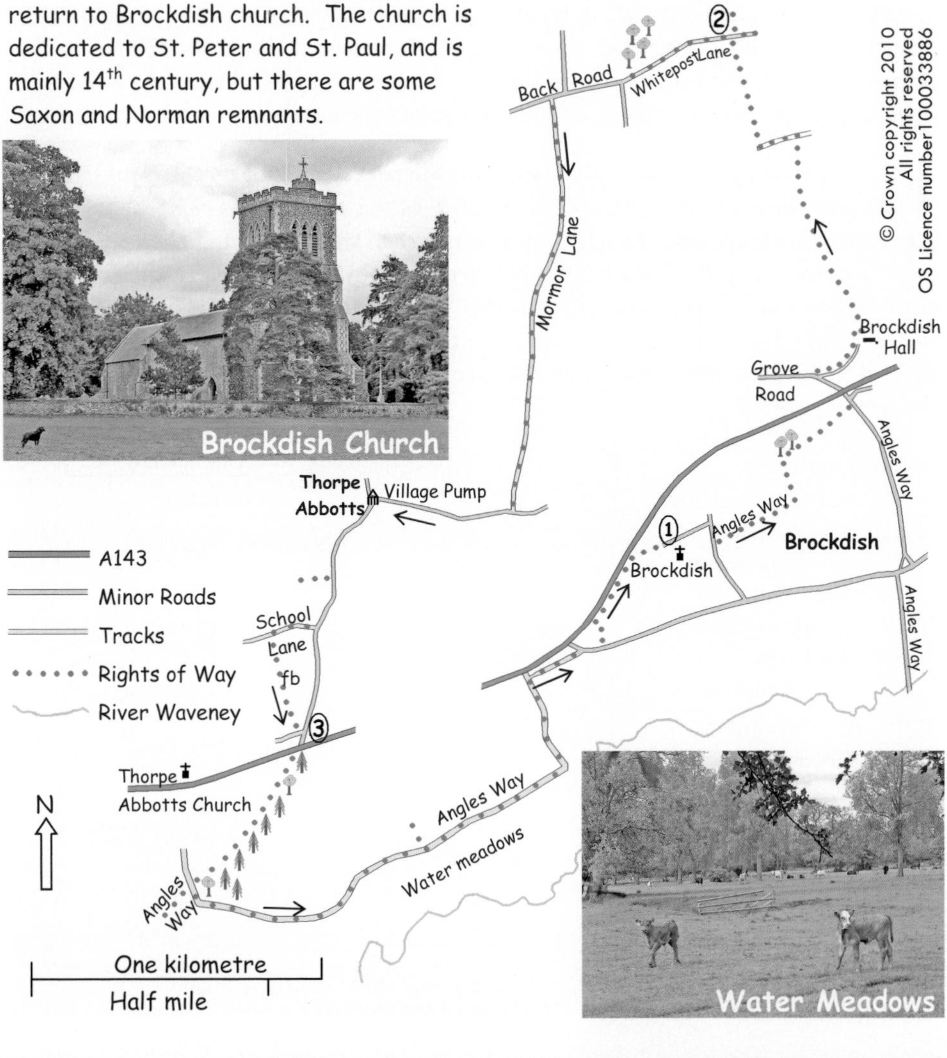

Brockdish Church

Back Road · Whitepost Lane · ② · Mormor Lane · Brockdish Hall · Grove Road · Angles Way

Thorpe Abbotts · Village Pump · ① Brockdish · Angles Way · **Brockdish** · Angles Way

A143
Minor Roads
Tracks
Rights of Way
River Waveney

School Lane · fb · ③

Thorpe Abbotts Church

N

Angles Way · Water meadows

One kilometre
Half mile

Water Meadows

12 Burston – Five and a half miles.   OS - L 144, E 230, Ref 137832

We start this walk from the Strike School in the centre of Burston – park on the school side of the driveway. In winter parts of the walk can be muddy. The school, which is on the edge of Church Green, next to St. Mary's Church, is set up as a small museum and a notice at the side entrance tells you where to find the key. You may visit any time during daylight hours, except Christmas or election days (it is used as a polling station), but note that each year on the first Sunday in September there is a rally and picnic with stalls on the Green and visitors from trade unions etc. The longest strike in history began in Burston on 1st April 1914 when Kitty and Tom Higdon, teachers at the nearby village school, were dismissed, their child-centred methods of education, years ahead of their time, were not popular with the local establishment. The children marched and sang in their support and the strike began – it lasted until August 1939. The first summer the children had lessons on the green, then in an old carpenters' shop, and funds were raised from a national appeal to build the new school which opened in 1917. For more information go to www.burstonstrikeschool.org.

1 Turn right along the road, continuing until the pavement ends on the right, turn left along Market Lane. Beyond the houses, as the track bends right, go left on a green track across a field, turn left at a corner then shortly right. Follow the left edge - at the end of the field cross a footbridge slightly to your right, then go ahead, over another footbridge, then left and right to continue along the field edge, then right and left to a stile and across the railway. Go ahead then left with the path under a power line. When you reach the road the path you need is just a little to the left.

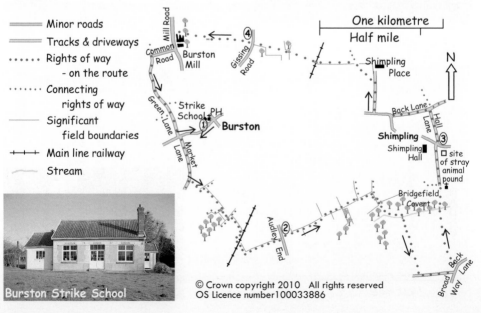

Minor roads
Tracks & driveways
Rights of way - on the route
Connecting rights of way
Significant field boundaries
Main line railway
Stream

One kilometre
Half mile

N

Mill Road
Common Road
Burston Mill
Gissing Road
Green Lane
Strike School
PH
Burston
Market Lane
Audley End
Shimpling Place
Back Lane
Hall Lane
Shimpling
Shimpling Hall
site of stray animal pound
Bridgefield Covert
Back Way Lane
Broad Lane

Burston Strike School

2 Go ahead for about 400 yards along a left edge, then with a field corner on your left, go through a gap to follow the path continuing the same line along a right edge. At the next boundary go ahead over a shallow ditch and continue ahead, and at a corner go right over a footbridge. You will see the next footbridge diagonally across the field in line with Shimpling Church, but the right of way follows the field edge. Cross the footbridge over a deep ditch then turn right to a corner and cross a bridge into Bridgefield Covert. Go ahead then bear left beside a stream and right over another bridge. Follow the field edge to a crossing track, turn left for 300 yards, and left again for a few yards along a road. Go left again onto a footpath, part of the Boudicca Way, across two fields towards Shimpling Church, crossing a footbridge (the same stream which flows through Bridgefield Covert). St. George's Church is now in the care of The Churches Conservation Trust - the oldest parts of the building date from the late 11th or early 12th centuries with 15th century alterations and additions. In the middle of the 17th century the angels' heads were sawn off the roof beams and other decoration destroyed by the Puritans. The round part of the tower is probably 12th century and the octagonal belfry 15th century. Beyond the church continue ahead to the road and cross into Hall Lane, formerly Partikyn's Lane after a 14th century parish chaplain. Behind you on the edge of the road is a notice marking the site of the stray animal pound before the enclosures of 1871. Burston and Shimpling have several of these notices commemorating parish history.

3 Continue for 300 yards, turn left on a crossing track which meets a road on a corner. Go ahead for about 120 yards, then right onto a footpath. The right of way goes diagonally left across a field before reaching Shimpling Place - it is possible to continue ahead a little further then walk round the field edges to the opposite point. Go through the gap in the field boundary and turn left under power lines along the field edge, cross the railway over a substantial brick bridge and go ahead across a field to a footbridge and pass to the left of a copse. The right of way is then diagonally right across the field aiming to the right of trees ahead, but you may prefer to use the track around the field edge. Follow the path along the edge of the trees out to a road.

4 Cross the road and continue on a path across fields, over a footbridge and go slightly right, avoiding a playing field to your left. Follow a narrow path, go over a crossing track, then, with Burston Mill on your left continue to another road. Turn left in front of the mill then turn right into Common Road. Burston Mill is on the site of an old windmill, now gone, but the large modern mill produces animal feed. At the end of the road turn left along Green Lane and then left along the road and back to the start. St. Mary's Church is adjacent to the Strike School. The tower fell down in the 18th century and now just the chancel is used for services and the nave is used as a hall. Kitty and Tom are buried in the churchyard.

13 Wreningham and Ashwellthorpe – Five and a half miles.

OS - L 144, E 237, Ref 149990

This walk starts from the small car park at the end of the public footpath through Long's Wood in Wreningham. The map shows how to find it if approaching from the B1113. The route through the wood was chosen for its simplicity and to include the old bridge over the "Swede and Swimmer" railway – clearly this was built to last as it has outlasted both the railway and a disused and overgrown track over the top. It remains as a monument to the unknown labourers who built both it and the railway, apparently on a diet of Norfolk stew with dumplings (swimmers). Sources vary as to whether the "Swedes" were Swedish labourers or the swedes which accompanied the dumplings in the stew, probably with not much else! Alternatively follow the waymarked route of the Ketts Country path, or devise your own route to arrive at the far corner of the wood (2). As well as Long's Wood the route also passes Lower Wood Ashwellthorpe. Both are two areas of deciduous woodland, both beautiful and managed to encourage wildlife and natural flora, but this is all they have in common. Long's was created in 1994 by a local landowner, with its wide grassy avenues it is open and light. Lower Wood, now in the care of Norfolk Naturalists Trust, is a remnant of the ancient wildwood that once covered much of England. It provided timber for local people for hundreds of years and supplied coppiced ash poles for the brush making industry in Wymondham.

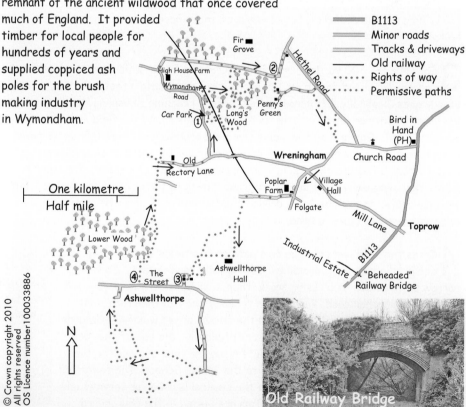

B1113
Minor roads
Tracks & driveways
Old railway
Rights of way
Permissive paths

Fir Grove
High House Farm
Wymondham Road
Car Park ①
Long's Wood
Penny's Green
Hethel Road
②
Bird in Hand (PH)
Wreningham
Church Road
Old Rectory Lane
Poplar Farm
Village Hall
Folgate
Mill Lane
Toprow
Industrial Estate
B1113
"Beheaded" Railway Bridge

One kilometre
Half mile

Lower Wood

④ The Street ③
Ashwellthorpe Hall
Ashwellthorpe

N

Old Railway Bridge

1 From the car park go via a gate in the right hand corner and follow the path until just round a left corner. Now either go down the steps to the old railway and left along the line, or stay on the top path. Either way at the fine brick railway bridge go right along a broad path. At a junction of paths, with a pond on your left, turn sharply left (almost right round the pond) and continue along the inside edge of the wood. After a right corner go soon left over a small footbridge and right along a wide track.

2 Just beyond the end of the wood and before the track turns to the left, turn right along the right edge of a field towards a cottage. *(If this path is too wet, continue on the track around the corner to meet a road by a house, turn right along the road for half a mile then right again to connect with the main route.)* At the field corner go through a gap, follow the path around the outside of a cottage garden and continue along the driveway, ignoring a turning to the right. As the drive turns to the left, just before a road, turn right into a field *(walkers who needed to avoid the wet field reconnect at this point and will turn left)*. This field was open access under the Stewardship Scheme until September 2009, but appears to be still available *(otherwise use the road and footpath as shown on the map)*, follow a clear diagonal path to the far corner, cross a stile and a footbridge, turn right along a field edge and continue to a road. Turn right, go over the cross roads in Wreningham and pass The Poplars on the right, turn right through the farmyard. Continue along the track to the end of wooden fencing and turn left. After about 270 yards the definitive path forks right across the open field, but you may continue along the field edge, turning right along the boundary of Ashwellthorpe Hall. It has early 17th century origins, but was much altered around 1840, and can be glimpsed through the trees. Continue along the field boundary and around left and right corners to reach a gap leading into the Ashwellthorpe churchyard via a footbridge over a moat. All Saints Church tower dates from the late 13th century and later centuries are well represented.

3 Go through to the road, turn left for about 200 yards, then right on a signed track at a bend. Continue to a junction of paths, turn sharp right on the nearer path. The route starts along the left hand field edge, but soon, just before a bend in the field boundary and a large tree, diverges diagonally across the field to join the right hand edge. Follow this over a crossing path, to a corner, pass a hump and turn right at a waymark post. Follow the path back to The Street, cross the road and turn right. Alternative routes between points 3 and 4 are shown on the map.

4 After 200 yards turn left opposite a 30 limit sign, and follow a right edge round to Lower Wood. If you are without a dog you may go through the wood, otherwise go right over a footbridge and follow the edge of the wood, turning left over another footbridge, keeping to the edge of the wood, turning left and right (the definitive path cuts the corner) then leaving the wood behind. Follow waymarks, going over a footbridge to change sides of the boundary, then further along the path moves back to the right again and you take a clear path across an open field. Cross another footbridge and bear round to the right along Old Rectory Lane to the road, and turn left back to the car park.

14 Hethel Bridge – Five and a three quarter miles.

OS - L 134+144. E 237, Ref 173993

This relatively short walk has much of interest to see on the way – do allow extra time. Start in the old cut-off section of road near Hethel Bridge - park close to or on the verge to avoid obstructing access for farm vehicles.

1 Walk westwards along the old road until just before it bends left, turn right onto a footpath over a stile in the hedge and go sharply right across the field to a footbridge and another stile. Continue in this direction, keeping to a right edge, and go over a third stile. Cross Cranes Road and go ahead along the left edge of a large field. As the path goes leftwards, crossing the hedge line, it then bears right into a narrow hedged path. When the path meets the road you may, if you wish, take a minor short cut, turning left along a track, but our preferred route is ahead along the road. Turn left on the pavement alongside the B1113 for a short distance.

2 Just beyond the war memorial turn left by a red telephone box, go diagonally across two fields to St Nicholas Church and over a stile into the churchyard. The church is in the care of The Historic Churches Preservation Trust and was open when we were there. There is no tower, but there is a bell round the back. The nave is 14th century and the chancel 15th century but a church was recorded in the Domesday Book. The Berney family have owned the manor since the mid 18th century and have a mausoleum in the church. Exit through the main gateway, turn left, and soon pass The Not So Old Old Rectory! The road bends left, then at a right bend, as the short cut track meets the road from the left, turn right onto a field edge path with woodland on the right. The path continues on the field edge beyond the wood, then, when it meets the corner of another wood turn left on a clear path with a ditch on the left. At the far side go ahead over a footbridge, follow the narrow path to a T junction, turn left and out onto the road, turn right and then soon left into Rectory Lane.

3 Pass the Moat House and continue to a field on the left and turn left along the edge, go over a stile, then diagonally right to cross another stile. The Hethel Thorn, an exceedingly small nature reserve, is to the right. It is only .025 hectares and consists of a single hawthorn, reputed to be over 700 years old. In 1841 the trunk measured over 12 feet (nearly four metres) in circumference and the spread of branches had a circumference of 31 yards (over 28 metres). Its best days may now be over, but it lives still and commands our respect and wonder. It is in the care of the Norfolk Naturalists Trust. From the Thorn turn back towards the fence and to the left of the church tower to a stile with a Kett's Country waymark pointing to a shingle drive and to All Saints Church on the left. The tower, probably Norman, is the oldest part of the church. There are several memorials to the Branthwaite family inside, landowners in the parish from about 1600 to 1750. The most splendid of these is the tomb of Myles Branthwaite who died in 1612 and it shows Myles, his wife Mary and their three surviving children, all carved in a muted pink alabaster.

4 Turn right from the church and continue ahead on the road, turn right at the end onto a track, then left on a clear track through the trees. Pass a field entrance on the right, cross a small clearing and turn left in the next small clearing, and soon left again by a post with a Stewardship Scheme map *(official access until September 2013)*. Follow a fence - the wood and beehives will be on the left and a field on the right - beyond the semi-circular bite out of the wood turn right on a tree lined green path. Cross a footbridge and turn right on a broad green track. Keep ahead, veering slightly left as a track joins from the right, then on via stiles and field edges to a driveway and follow this to Potash Lane; turn left and continue to the B1135.

5 Cross the road and turn left and soon right on a footpath opposite Corporation Farmhouse. The path starts to the right of a watercourse, changes sides, but continues ahead to Hethel Road; turn left for 150 yards. Turn right onto a track, but almost immediately, as the track turns to the right, go left into a field. This field was open access under the Stewardship Scheme until September 2009, but appears to be still available *(otherwise use the road and footpath as shown on the map)*. There is a clear diagonal path to the far corner, cross a stile and a footbridge, turn right along a field edge and go left along the road. Continue ahead past the left junction and All Saints Church. At the Bird in Hand PH go straight across the B1135 onto a footpath, following a right edge. At the field corner bear right down some rough steps and follow the short winding path to a footbridge over a stream, cross, go ahead across a narrow field and turn left alongside the fence. Go under the road via a tunnel, bear right across the small field, over a stile and back to the start.

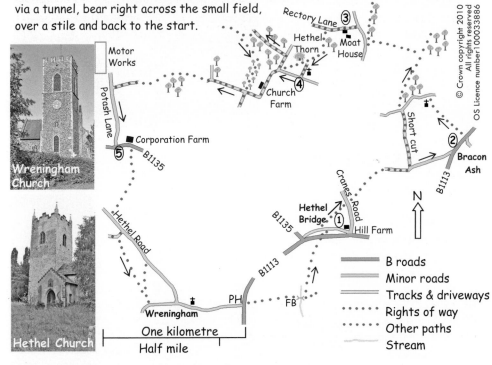

Motor Works

Potash Lane

Corporation Farm

Wreningham Church

Hethel Church

Rectory Lane **(3)**

Hethel Thorn

Moat House

Church Farm

(4)

Short cut

(2)

Bracon Ash

B1113

Cranes Road

B1135

Hethel Bridge **(1)**

Hill Farm

N

Hethel Road

B1113

Wreningham

PH

FB

One kilometre

Half mile

B roads
Minor roads
Tracks & driveways
Rights of way
Other paths
Stream

15 Burgh next Aylsham – Five and three-quarter miles.
OS - L 134, E 238+OL40, Ref 218250

There is space to park in front of the church. This is a wonderful walk for lovers of wildlife. In summer the river abounds with dragon flies, and kingfishers may be seen if you are lucky. Please remember to respect the countryside and the wildlife and farm animals that live in this special landscape. When the Bure Valley narrow gauge railway service is running you might adapt the walk to combine it with a ride on the train which runs between Aylsham and Wroxham. Either Brampton or Buxton station would be convenient (you could use both and shorten the walk a little).

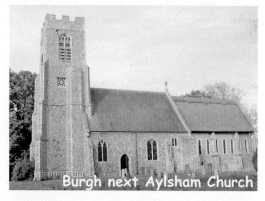
Burgh next Aylsham Church

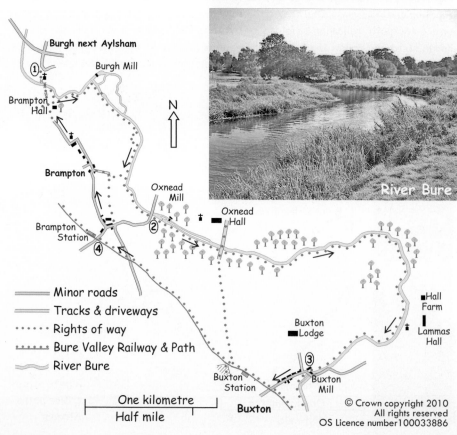
River Bure

Minor roads
Tracks & driveways
········ Rights of way
········ Bure Valley Railway & Path
River Bure

One kilometre
Half mile

1 Start at St. Mary's Church. Go through the churchyard to the back and cross two wooden footbridges into a meadow where you turn immediately left to gain the river bank. Follow the river bank path until you reach a right hand bend with views across to a former water mill. Keep following the bank of the river, past a weir and into a small copse. If the river is high parts of this path may come close to the water level so take care of your footing. Beyond the copse cross a stile into another meadow where there are wonderful views across the surrounding countryside. Keep going ahead crossing several more stiles until you reach a road bridge over the river.

2 Cross the road either by going through a gate on your right or by climbing over a stile at the side of the bridge; then over a stile on the opposite side to take you into another field. The fields on both sides of the road may contain some handsome horses from a nearby stud including delightful small Haflinger horses. These were first introduced into this country from Austria in the 1960s and originate from crossing the native Tyrolean ponies with Arab horses. You may also see swans here. As you continue along this stretch of the river you will see on the opposite bank firstly Oxnead Mill then glimpses through the trees of Oxnead Hall with its lovely gardens. Just after the hall cross a track. Keeping the river on your left walk along the river bank as the river turns right in a broad sweep. Eventually you will see views of Lammas Hall and Church (where Anna Sewell author of "Black Beauty" is buried) and after another half mile you reach Buxton Mill where the path leaves the river.

3 Keeping the Mill on your left go through to Mill Street and turn right, passing cottages until you reach a railway bridge. Do not go under, but climb the steps to reach a path at the side of the railway track, now the narrow gauge Bure Valley Railway. Turn right on the path with the track on your left, go past Buxton Station, then continue until you reach Brampton Station. The trackside walking and cycling route follows the whole nine miles of the railway.

4 Take the steps down to the road at this point and turn left at a road sign to Upper Brampton. After some houses the road bends right, and then left; go past the Village Hall on the right ignoring any footpath signs on the way. Shortly you will reach St. Peter's Church Brampton with its interesting octagonal tower. Either cut the corner of the road by going through the churchyard or follow the road round towards a sign saying "Farm Traffic Only". Go ahead through a gate on to a track which soon leads to a footpath sloping down to a footbridge. Cross the footbridge, then go through a gate ignoring a second bridge on the left. Go ahead and in a few yards you reach the back of Burgh next Aylsham Church. If you did not fully appreciate the attractions of its setting before your walk, you now have another opportunity! The unusual chancel of St. Mary's dates from the early 13th century and although it has been restored it is little altered. It is light and airy with beautiful simplicity. The steps down from the nave to the chancel, which now strike us as rather different, were apparently usual in medieval times. Certainly the church is well worth a visit, both inside and out.

16 Rushall, Dickleburgh and Lonely Road - Six miles.
OS - L 156, E 230, Ref 198827

Lonely Road, running between Dickleburgh and Rushall, was shown on Faden's map of Norfolk published in 1797, but was undoubtedly in existence long before that date. It was in use until shortly before World War 1 when it was closed for safety reasons because of airships at the Pulham Air Station. It was partially reopened between the Wars, but closed again at the beginning of World War 2 - the middle section completely obliterated - until about 2007 when it was reopened as a bridle-way. For a long time the two ends of Lonely Road, named on 1:25000 OS maps, have looked very lonely indeed with no link between them! Now, even though the maps have not yet been updated, the link has been recreated and it opens up possibilities for new walks. Although this walk includes rather more road walking than we would normally choose, there are attractive views, some fine hedges and usually very little traffic. The off-road paths and tracks, including Hollow Lane and the path by Oliver's and Dodd's Woods in addition to Lonely Road, are a delight. We start this walk at St. Mary's Church Rushall where there is limited parking when no service in progress.

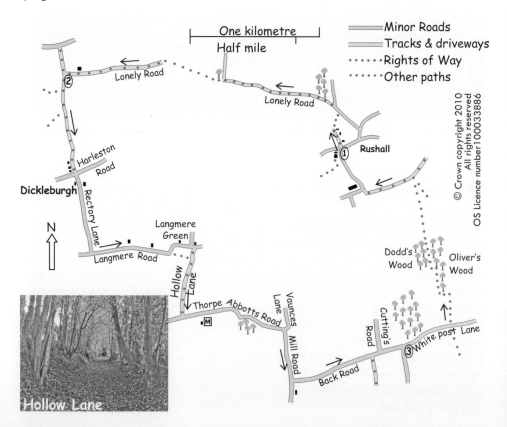

1 With your back towards the church go left to the junction and straight across to a farm track and through two gates. Continue until just beyond the farm sheds and through a gateway, then turn sharply right to a stile (at the time of writing hidden behind a skip). Go diagonally across a field to another stile and out to a road. Turn left and continue ahead along Lonely Road when the motor road turns to the right. Keep to the track, but when it turns to the right continue ahead across a large field. The right of way bears just a little to the right, towards a gap to the right of a line of trees on the far side of the field. Go slightly left into the tree lined track – this is the western end of Lonely Road. Be careful of the stumps sticking up through the surface. It was previously very overgrown and the stumps will probably remain for quite a long time, indeed they may get worse as the soil around them erodes a little.

2 Just beyond a house with a large garden, the main track turns sharply right, but our route takes a lesser track to the left across a field. Just before this path bends to the right, go through the field boundary to the left, then continue ahead on the same line as previously to Harleston Road. Go across into Rectory Lane, then left at the end along Langmere Road. When this bends to the left, go ahead on a path across Langmere Green, choose the right fork, then right into Hollow Lane which has an air of great antiquity. The lane leads to Thorpe Abbotts Road, turn left, and soon pass the 100th Bomb Group Memorial Museum, which commemorates the US Air Force presence at Thorpe Abbotts during WW2. The museum is closed in midwinter, but a board at the entrance displays the opening times. Continue to a junction with Vaunces Lane and turn right to Mill Road and take the first turning on the left along Back Road. Ignore Cuttings Road on the left and continue ahead to a right-angled corner and go straight ahead along a track, Whitepost Lane.

3 After about a quarter of a mile a waymarked path goes to the right and a few yards beyond this point our route turns to the left along a right edge and continues to a crossing boundary. Turn left towards Oliver's Wood and follow it's southern edge then right along it's western edge. When the path enters Dodd's Wood, turn left for a few yards then right again. As the path leaves the wood it goes to the right of the field boundary ahead, but after about 250 yards turns left across a footbridge then right to follow the other side of the boundary. Turn left on a crossing track, follow this around to the right and out to a road, go ahead back to the church. St. Mary's may have Saxon origins and it has a round tower with an eight sided Perpendicular top. The chancel is Early English.

Rushall Church

17 Peddars Way, Merton and Pockthorpe - Six miles.
OS - L 144, E 229, Ref 906966

This walk starts from the old Tottington road, close to the Peddars Way crossing, just before the closure point, where there is space to park alongside the road. There is a war memorial, set well back, on the corner where this road leaves the through road from Pockthorpe to Watton. The route follows an attractive section of the Peddars Way through Merton Park, with some fine old trees. If you choose late March or early April you can expect a fine display of daffodils.

1 Turn north along the Peddars Way. The first 1½ miles of the walk follows the boundary of the Stanford Battle Area, taken over for military training during WW2 as a temporary measure, but extended indefinitely. Tottington was one of the lost villages. At a stone slab with carved lettering (only just readable) bear left with the path then right through wooden rails. Keep ahead following the track, then through a gate near a lodge, pass Home Farm and continue to a crossroads. The Peddars Way turns left, but go ahead on the alternative bridleway route. (For a shorter option turn right along the road to Merton). The track becomes narrower and continues as a path.

2 At a field corner the bridle route goes ahead over a footbridge, but turn right on a footpath along the field edge. Turn right along a road and continue to Merton, pass the shelter on the village green (given by local people to commemorate the Queen's Silver Jubilee in 1977) and turn left at the junction. Soon, on a bend in the road, go right along a public footpath. Bear left along Sally's Walk, a delightful path through woodland, back into Merton Park. Turn left along a track; you may then visit the church, before going through the white gate to the road. St. Peter's is a small flint church with a round tower. The phone number of the key holder is shown in the north porch. Although the nave and chancel are early 14th century, the tower is Saxon or early Norman, but there is evidence that the original church predated the tower. There is a fine early 14th century screen. On the wall beside the 17th century double-decker pulpit there is a brass depicting William de Grey, who died in

Merton Church

1495 – he is shown with his two wives, five sons and five daughters. Another brass, of Thomas de Grey died 1562, is in the floor of the large Jacobean box pew. Looking south from the churchyard there is a fine view over the park and large round pond, the remaining wing of Merton Hall (much was destroyed by a fire in 1956) and the 17th century gatehouse. Turn right along the road and continue to the junction by the war memorial.

3 The Tottington war memorial commemorates both those who were lost and those who returned from WW1. It was originally situated in Tottington village, but was moved to its present site after WW2 – we hope that the Tottington men lost in that war are commemorated on the war memorials of other villages. The shortest option is to turn right and straight back to the start, but it would be pity to miss the pretty woodland route from Pockthorpe. For this longer route go ahead to a crossroads, turn right through Pockthorpe and continue ahead on a footpath beyond the village street. Ignoring a track to the left, go ahead then round to the right by a stile.

Follow the path through woodland and across a field, go over a stile and turn left along the road back to the start.

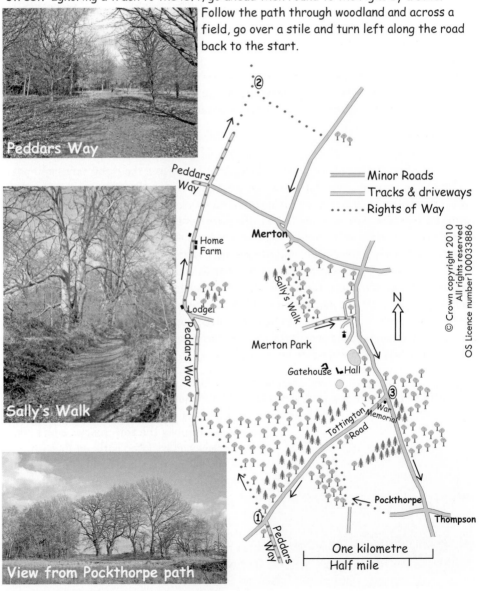

Peddars Way

Sally's Walk

View from Pockthorpe path

Peddars Way

Peddars Way

Home Farm

Lodge

Merton

Sally's Walk

Peddars Way

Merton Park

Gatehouse Hall

Tottington Road

War Memorial

Pockthorpe

Thompson

Peddars Way

N

Minor Roads
Tracks & driveways
Rights of Way

One kilometre
Half mile

18 Castle Acre and Newton - Six miles.

OS - L 132, E 236/238, Ref 817151

Castle Acre has everything a historic village could wish for, including the ruins of a castle and a priory, a fine parish church and many attractive old houses. The Peddars Way, a Roman road, crosses the river Nar and passes through the village; it is now a National Trail, a long distance walk, from Knettishall Heath on the Norfolk/Suffolk border to Holme next the Sea. The Cluniac Priory and the Norman Castle are in the care of English Heritage; there is a charge for admission to the Priory. The Priory ruins are still magnificent and the setting beautiful. The Castle is one of the finest motte and bailey earthworks in the country. St. James's Church is Perpendicular, large and impressive, a reflection of the importance and wealth of the 14th century town. Although this walk can easily be completed in half a day, it is well worth spending the rest of the day exploring the village. There are good pubs and tearooms. Start in the village centre, alongside Stocks Green, adjacent to the High Street,

1 Walk westwards along the High Street, then turn left into the churchyard, keeping by the eastern edge. Continue ahead on the path past allotments. Bear left along Chimney Street, after Blind Lane joins from the right, turn right on to Bailey Street and cross the bridge over the Nar. When the wider road swings to the right Bailey Street continues ahead as a narrow lane, but there is the option of using a permissive path, provided under the Environmental Stewardship Scheme, along the field edge on the left (clamber up the grassy bank). Both the lane and the path emerge together at the A1065. Go straight across to another lane, then step over a low earth bank on the left to another permissive field edge path. This path continues close to the lane for half a kilometre then meets the end of a right of way which diverges from the lane with a wooded area between lane and path. Continue on the path to a minor road, cross and go ahead along Ruckold's Lane, a grassy track. At the end of a small wooded area, Wells Green, turn sharp left at a T junction, keep ahead, ignoring a field edge path to the right.

2 Bear left along a road and then keep to the right at a junction. Just before the A1065 turn right along a track in front of the Manor House. Continue to Winchester Hill and follow the path round to the left on the far side of the field

Newton Millpond

boundary. Initially the path follows a left edge then becomes an enclosed path; go through a gate and follow the track across Grove Common. Go straight across the A1065 and down steps to a footpath across a field and over a low fence. Turn left along a track, join a driveway, continue to a lane, turn right, cross a bridge by Newton Mill and the millpond. Continue round to the left following St. James Road over Newton Common.

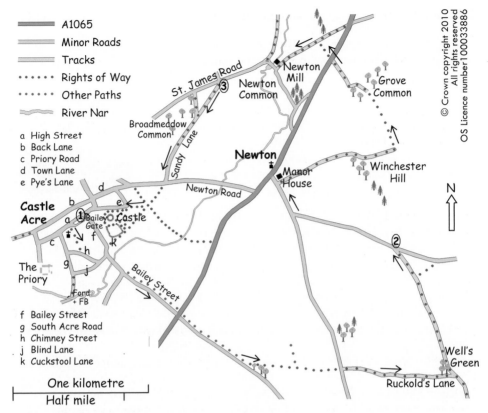

A1065
Minor Roads
Tracks
· · · · · Rights of Way
· · · · · Other Paths
River Nar

a High Street
b Back Lane
c Priory Road
d Town Lane
e Pye's Lane

Castle Acre

The Priory

f Bailey Street
g South Acre Road
h Chimney Street
j Blind Lane
k Cuckstool Lane

St. James Road
Broadmeadow Common
Sandy Lane
Newton Common
Newton Mill
Grove Common
Newton
Manor House
Winchester Hill
Newton Road
Bailey Street
Ford + FB
Well's Green
Ruckold's Lane

N

One kilometre
Half mile

3 Continue to crossing tracks and take the fork on the left, keep ahead along the edge of Broadmeadow Common. The track becomes a minor lane. At a T junction go straight across and through a gate to follow a path going a little to the right. At crossing paths go through a gate onto the fenced path by houses, initially going straight ahead, but almost immediately bearing right. Continue to a corner, go a

little to the right and out to a road by the castle car park. The short route back into the village is straight along Pyes Lane, but a meandering route around the castle may be preferred. On re-entering the village note the Bailey Gate, a remnant of the old town walls, still spanning the road from the south. You may well have passed through it when you first arrived in Castle Acre.

Castle Acre - view from the motte.

19 Thetford – Six miles with shorter options. OS - L 144, E 229, ref 866812

Although this walk is centred on Thetford and goes through the town twice, only about half a mile of the route is along town streets. The remainder includes commons, the British Trust for Ornithology nature reserve around Nunnery Lakes, the historic sites of Thetford Castle and St. Mary's 12th century Cluniac Priory and pretty riverside walks. Start from the car park on the east side of theA134 on Barnhamcross Common.   For a rather shorter walk start from the car park by Nuns' Bridges opposite Mill Lane, from the bus station or one of the other town centre car parks.

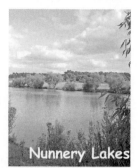
Nunnery Lakes

1 Head northwards over the common with the A134 to the left, choosing your own route, but if you follow the eastern boundary, the path will pass through woodland – in which case when the Little Ouse comes into view on the right (with a seat) turn sharp left, then bear round to the right, with a pumping station on the right. As the Common narrows, all paths join Nuns' Bridges Road. Continue ahead alongside the road then turn right into Nunnery Place. Pass the BTO offices (the gardens are open to the public during office hours) and continue beyond Nightingale Way, along a track over two bridges, then soon right through a kissing gate. Follow the path to a fork with a seat (there is a seat with a better view further round). Choose either path; the route goes right round the first lake with a short diversion alongside the western edge of the second lake to a bird hide. The landscaped lakes are old gravel workings. Along the route are interesting interpretative boards with information about the flora, fauna, formation of the lakes and changes to the river system. Return to the kissing gate, turn briefly left, then immediately before the bridge, turn right to follow the riverside path.

2 Just before the path reaches a big kissing gate and a footbridge (leading to the Nuns' Bridges car park) turn right to follow a woodland and riverside path. Turn briefly left along Arlington Way, cross Castle Street, pass through a gap in the fence, go left over the old bridge on Melford Common and continue ahead. On reaching Green Lane cross back over Castle Street, pass a children's playground and continue across Castle Meadow. Follow the tarmac path between the castle mound and the ramparts. The Norman motte, constructed within Iron Age fortifications, is the second largest earthwork in the country, only Silbury Hill is larger. *You may continue ahead to turn right along Castle Lane for a pleasant diversion to visit the Forgotten Garden in the grounds of Ford Place (open Thursday to Sunday all year).* Otherwise bear round to the right before reaching Castle Lane to follow a sunken path, firstly with a wall and then a fence to the left. Turn left on a clear path then up a slope, through a gap in a wall, turn right along Rampart Way then left along Castle Street. At a roundabout continue ahead along King Street. Keep ahead via the pedestrian route into Minstergate, pass the Charles Burrell Museum, then through the subway leading to the Priory.

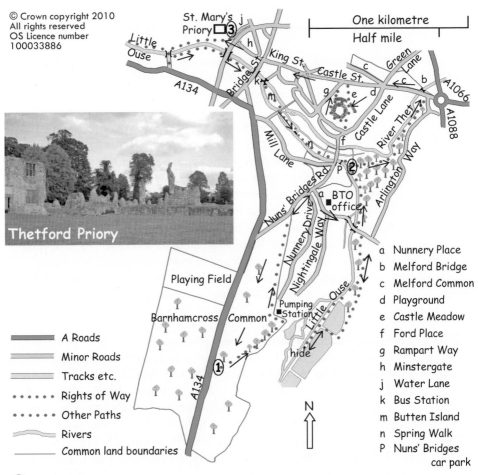

Thetford Priory

One kilometre
Half mile

a Nunnery Place
b Melford Bridge
c Melford Common
d Playground
e Castle Meadow
f Ford Place
g Rampart Way
h Minstergate
j Water Lane
k Bus Station
m Butten Island
n Spring Walk
P Nuns' Bridges
car park

━━━ A Roads
═══ Minor Roads
▭▭▭ Tracks etc.
• • • • • Rights of Way
• • • • • Other Paths
〜〜 Rivers
——— Common land boundaries

N

3 Go briefly left along Water Lane, then either turn right to visit the Priory ruins, or immediately take the path ahead, soon with the river to the left. As the path bears to the right continue ahead along the river bank to a bridge, cross and turn left along the Haling path to the Town Bridge. Cross Bridge Street and continue along the river and edge of the bus station and car park and cross a three pronged bridge, turning right in the middle of it onto Butten Island. Turn right along Bridges Walk, then left following the sign to Nuns' Bridges via Spring Walk. Turn right along the road, pass the ends of Nunnery Place and Nunnery Drive and then make your way back over Barnhamcross Common choosing a different route to the outward one, being careful not to overshoot the car park – unless you actually wish to extend the walk.

Little Ouse

20 Saxlingham Nethergate – Six miles. OS - L 134, E 237, ref 234969

This walk starts from the car park for the recreation ground and playing field in Saxlingham Nethergate. The landscape is undulating with attractive vistas, many of the fields have fine hedges and there are areas of mature woodland.

1 From the recreation ground turn right along the road, pass the very narrow Hall Lane, then turn right through the churchyard. St. Mary the Virgin, which is usually open, is largely Perpendicular, though the north aisle is a Victorian addition. A particular feature is the stained glass, much of which is medieval and includes some of the oldest in Norfolk; it was restored 50 years ago, but not set in the original positions, indeed some originated from the ruined Saxlingham Thorpe Church half a mile to the south. The clock in the tower dates from 1794. Go to the left of the church to a gate at the rear then keep ahead along a field edge. As path turns to the left go right over a stile. Continue ahead between fields to a corner on a road, go ahead for a few yards and follow round to the left, then turn right into Wash Lane. This Wash Lane is just in Shotesham - we will meet another one, in Saxlingham, later in the walk.

2 Just before reaching an old barn, (marked on OS map as Low Farm) turn right along a footpath to follow a left edge and over a footbridge at the first field boundary. Continue to follow the left edge, ignoring a footpath to the left, bear right with the field boundary as it curves around. At the end of the field turn right, keeping to the edge then follow the path through a strip of woodland to the road. Cross the road and go along the track very slightly to the right. Turn right at the "Private Woodland Keep Out" sign. Go ahead leaving the woodland behind, ignore a turning to the left and keep ahead until you reach more woodland ahead. *(At this point you may opt for a shorter option by turning right and soon left to follow the east/west paths shown on the map, rejoining the main route at 5.)*

3 Otherwise turn left over a footbridge. Follow the right edge to another corner, turn left for a few yards to join another corner, then turn right through a gap in the hedge and over another footbridge. The path follows a right edge, but after crossing a footbridge transfers to the other side and then continues following the left edge. Go ahead across an open field, then through a gap onto a hedged path, then join a track and out to a minor road. Turn right and soon right again through Hempnall.

4 At the war memorial turn left along Fairstead Lane. Pass Krons Manor, then opposite a road called The Krons turn right along the driveway for Fairstead Lane Farm. Just beyond the farm buildings and farmhouse, Pymar's Lane, a grassy track, goes to the left. When the track forks at a small wood, keep to the right. Follow the woodland path and well-hedged track as it bends left and right.

Ruined Church

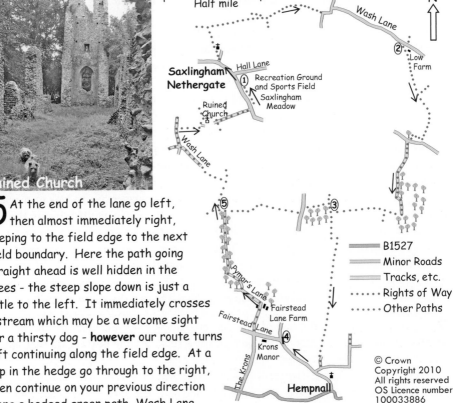

One kilometre
Half mile

N

Saxlingham Nethergate

Hall Lane

Recreation Ground and Sports Field

Saxlingham Meadow

Ruined Church

Wash Lane

① ② ③ ④ ⑤

Low Farm

Wash Lane

Pymar's Lane

Fairstead Lane

Fairstead Lane Farm

The Krons

Krons Manor

Hempnall

═══ B1527
═══ Minor Roads
═══ Tracks, etc.
•••• Rights of Way
••••• Other Paths

5 At the end of the lane go left, then almost immediately right, keeping to the field edge to the next field boundary. Here the path going straight ahead is well hidden in the trees - the steep slope down is just a little to the left. It immediately crosses a stream which may be a welcome sight for a thirsty dog - **however** our route turns left continuing along the field edge. At a gap in the hedge go through to the right, then continue on your previous direction along a hedged green path, Wash Lane.

When the path forks, turn right, then after about 150 yards turn right again over a footbridge and go across a field. Turn left, ignore the first path on your right, then at a junction with Boudica's Way turn right along a path with woodland on the right and a field left. The remains of Saxlingham Thorpe church, also dedicated to St. Mary, are hidden in the woodland, it was abandoned over 200 years ago, probably due to diminishing population.   Bear left when you meet a stony track and follow it to the road. Turn left for a few yards, then turn right into Saxlingham Meadows and continue parallel with the road back to the playing field.   The Meadows are owned by Saxlingham Parish Council and managed by the Playing Field Committee. A new orchard and other trees have been planted. The meadows are a haven for wildlife, wild flowers proliferate and as the trees mature the whole area will become even more beautiful. Winding paths are mown through the whole site; our route takes the direct line along the edge, but if you have time and energy you may like to explore further.

St. Mary the Virgin

21 Redgrave Fen and Bressingham - Six and a half miles.
OS - L 144, E 230, Ref 053803

This walk starts from the car park at Redgrave Fen and follows a route around the eastern part of the Fen including a section of the Angles Way, then by contrast loops round to the north using quiet lanes and field paths. The Fen, a National Nature Reserve, is open daily; the visitor centre is open at weekends and during school holidays. The route includes two paths which illustrate the difficulties caused by incomplete changes to the rights of way system – the original, legal, routes remain on the map, but do not coincide with the practical walking routes. How are strangers, even with good map reading abilities, expected to find their way around? Both are in section two. The first, at the beginning, is the route, originally a little further south, crossing the Hundred River, but not accessible for many years due to lack of a bridge. The new route overcame this difficulty, a bridge was installed and the line of the path made more convenient for the landowners, but the legal processes started around 1999/2000 have not been completed! The second case is the path from Halford Lane, apparently "moved" without attempting to even start the legal processes. If the definitive path, from the first bend in the lane, is made clearly available again, this should be used, but in the meantime you may choose to use the route described below.

1 Go through a gate to the left of the Visitor Centre, then left through another gate, follow the path ahead then go right at a fork. At the bottom, go through a gate and left along the river bank to the second bridge, but turn left away from the river, go over a stile (with dog gate) following the Waveney Trail, over another stile and a bridge, ignore a kissing gate on the left and continue ahead. Pass Lang Fen Cottage and go ahead along the road.

2 Turn right on a footpath just before the road bends right. The stile has a small gate on top, so it is not quite as tall as may initially appear, but lacks access for dogs. *(For an alternative route with a large dog, continue on the road around the corner, cross a bridge with white rails and turn immediately right on a short track to join the footpath just east of the footbridge).* Go across a field to another stile and footbridge, continue ahead along a left edge, over a footbridge by a house and turn right along Fen Street to the gates of Three Gates Farm. Turn left, cross the

A1066, continue along Halford Lane, go around left and right bends. Turn right on a permissive path (signed as "Public Footpath") along a field boundary, turn left at field corner and keep to the edge, go just to the left of a gate, over a footbridge and continue ahead. Turn right the along road, ignore a path on the right, bear left along Fersfield Road, continue to another junction and turn left into Hall Lane.

Three Gates

3 Just beyond Willow Farm turn left along a cross field path (finger post opposite, under a tree); soon join a field edge, then at a field corner bear right and almost immediately left over a footbridge into a green lane. Turn right along a road, pass Walnut Tree Farm, turn left along a signed path over two footbridges, go along a field edge, cross a track and continue to the A1066. Cross and turn right along the verge then left into Pooley Street following the road round to the left, overlapping 100 yards used on the outward route.

4 Turn right on a signed path between horse paddocks and over two footbridges, go along a field edge, then from a corner go across an arable field (alternatively round the left edge.) Go through a gap, along the edge of a garden to join a drive-way and out to Brickkiln Lane. Turn briefly right, then left along a footpath *(if you find this path overgrown you may turn left along the lane and follow it back to Redgrave Fen)*. Turn left by a field corner on a crossing path and follow this to another lane, turn right, round a left bend then left along Low Common Road and back to the start.

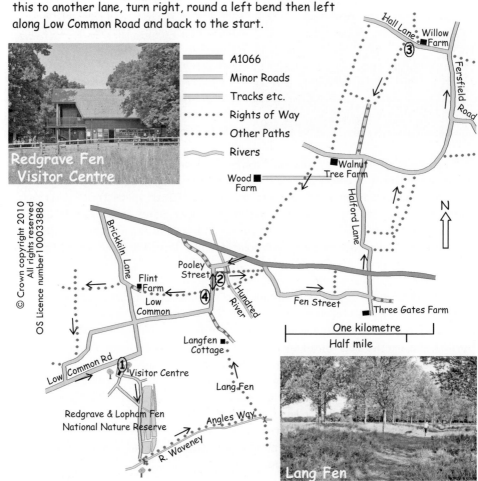

Redgrave Fen Visitor Centre

A1066
Minor Roads
Tracks etc.
Rights of Way
Other Paths
Rivers

Hall Lane
Willow Farm
3
Fersfield Road
Walnut Tree Farm
Wood Farm
Halford Lane
N

Brickkiln Lane
Flint Farm
Pooley Street
2
Low Common
4
Hundred River
Fen Street
Three Gates Farm

One kilometre
Half mile

Langfen Cottage
Low Common Rd
1 Visitor Centre
Lang Fen
Redgrave & Lopham Fen National Nature Reserve
Angles Way
R. Waveney

Lang Fen

22 Sheringham - Six and a half miles.   OS - L 133, E 252, Ref 156435

Start by the children's play area opposite the Burlington Hotel.   There is parking on The Lees.

1 Proceed down to the promenade and turn right.   Follow the promenade, passing the mural and plaques which are part of the Sheringham Art and Sculpture Trail. At the mural depicting local birds, take the left hand, lower route.   Soon leave the sea front where the promenade turns right, keeping the mural of a ship wreck on your left. Proceed inland along Beach Road and Beeston Road, then take the third left into Priory Road. Turn immediately right along a path beside a stream. Continue to Curtis Lane, turn right and under a bridge. Immediately after the bridge, turn

left on a path beside the stream. Continue to Brook Road, go ahead, keeping the common on your right. The road surface changes to gravel as it passes Meadow Cottages on the left; soon turn right at the signed bridleway to Beeston Regis Priory which dates back to Magna Carta. Follow the bridleway, cross the main road, turn right, following the pavement to a lay-by opposite Priory Maze.

Beeston Regis Priory

2 Turn left into the lay-by, then left along a path onto Beeston Common with many rare specimens of animal and plant life. Continue along the path, signed to Shering Wood, and at the pond turn left, waymarked "Sheringham Trail". Just past a seat on the left, go ahead ignoring a path to the right. After about $1/4$ mile, at a junction, take the right fork, follow the path as it bends to the west and continue for another $1/3$ mile, then at a waymark pointing right, leave the Sheringham Trail and take the narrow path ahead towards a holly bush on your left. The path soon turns southwards, widens, and becomes an unsurfaced road as it passes a house on the right. Pass more houses and continue to a 'T' junction and turn right up the hill. At the end of the road follow the path ahead, keeping the fence on your left.   At the end of the fence take the wide path to the right, downhill into woodland. At the bottom, keeping the small wired enclosure to your right, join a track ahead. Turn right, the enclosure still on the right. Keep ahead for $1/4$ mile, ignoring paths to right and left, then at crossing paths with a low stone marker on your left, with lettering 'SG WCo 1934', take the clear path climbing to your left. Pass a pond on the right, and soon fork right, again following the 'Sheringham Trail' until you reach a waymark where the path passes either side of a mature oak tree. Take the path forking right, keeping to the right side of a grassed picnic area.   Emerge from the picnic area through a gap in the hedge.

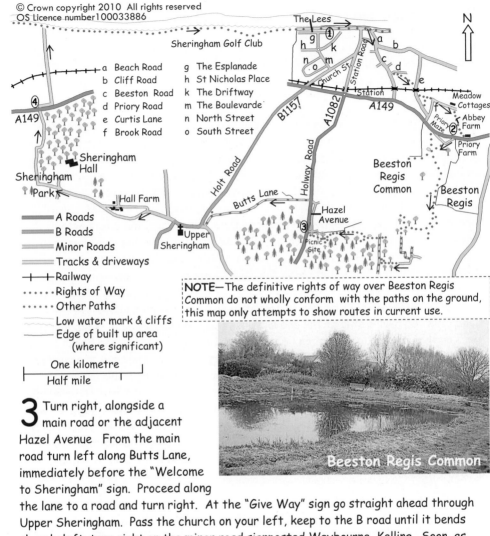

a Beach Road
b Cliff Road
c Beeston Road
d Priory Road
e Curtis Lane
f Brook Road

g The Esplanade
h St Nicholas Place
k The Driftway
m The Boulevarde
n North Street
o South Street

━━ A Roads
━━ B Roads
━━ Minor Roads
━━ Tracks & driveways
+—+— Railway
..... Rights of Way
..... Other Paths
～～ Low water mark & cliffs
— Edge of built up area
   (where significant)

One kilometre
Half mile

NOTE—The definitive rights of way over Beeston Regis Common do not wholly conform with the paths on the ground, this map only attempts to show routes in current use.

Beeston Regis Common

3 Turn right, alongside a main road or the adjacent Hazel Avenue From the main road turn left along Butts Lane, immediately before the "Welcome to Sheringham" sign. Proceed along the lane to a road and turn right. At the "Give Way" sign go straight ahead through Upper Sheringham. Pass the church on your left, keep to the B road until it bends sharply left, turn right on the minor road signposted Weybourne, Kelling. Soon, as this bends right, go ahead along a "no through road", over a cattle grid, and into Sheringham Park. Follow the drive through the park, crossing another cattle grid, until you see Sheringham Hall on your right. The Hall and park were owned by the Upcher family from 1811 until 1987, when it was sold to the National Trust. At the junction in front of the Hall continue ahead on the track towards a gate, go through and turn right, following the track to the main road.

4 Cross, take the track to the right and then left to the cliff top. Turn right and make your way back towards Sheringham. Before returning to the start point in front of the Burlington Hotel, note the compass made from redundant sea defences

23 Mendham, Homersfield and Redenhall – Seven miles.
OS - L 156, E 230, Ref 271829

This walk uses part of the Angles Way between Mendham and Homersfield, just in Suffolk (the county boundary follows the river); the route returns along paths and tracks on the Norfolk side. Start at the car park in the centre of Mendham.

1 Turn right out of the car park and left at the cross roads. Continue past a lane on the right and soon left over a stile. Follow the left edge into a narrow section of the field, where it can be rather wet. Go through a gateway or over a stile, then bear slightly right across a field (although skirting round to the left may avoid a wet area) to a footbridge. Cross the stream and go over a narrow field to a stile, cross and turn left. Keep in this direction, just above the flood plain on the left. Pass through gates or over stiles and just beyond Downs Farm turn sharp left onto a track. At a gateway leave the track to follow a narrow path on the right between track and bank and over a stile, or go straight up the bank, left along the top and through a gap in the fence just above the stile – either of these manoeuvres avoids a section of the track which is frequently very wet. Turn right following the field edge, then over a stile in a corner to a woodland path, once again just above the flood plain. Go over a stile at the end and out to a road and turn left. Keep left at a junction then right at a T junction. After about 100 yards, as the road bends to the right, turn sharp left along a bridleway to St. Mary's Church. Continue to a road and turn left, then right, over the green, past the Black Swan public house and continue to Homersfield Bridge. This bridge, originally for all traffic and a main crossing of the Waveney between Suffolk and Norfolk, is now only open as a footbridge. It was built at a cost of £344 in the early 1870s and the construction was very technically advanced at the time; the framework over the arch is encased in concrete, a forerunner of modern reinforced concrete. It was restored in the 1990s - that cost around £85,000.

2 Cross the bridge, turn left along the B1062, then right onto the A143. Cross the road via the refuge, continue past the Dove Restaurant then turn sharp left. At the very top of the hill and just before a house on the right turn left along a footpath. Follow the fence round to the left, then, after seventy or eighty yards go right over a footbridge and continue ahead to Tunbeck Road. Turn right, then immediately left along Stony Lane, continue until the main track bends very sharply to the right, keep ahead either through a ford or over an adjacent footbridge. In a few yards turn left over a stile beside a gate and follow the left edge of two fields alongside a watercourse and a wood. At a field corner go a little to the right, then left along a short track through the trees, then turn right at a junction. Redenhall church is now in view across the fields on the left. When the track bends to the right keep straight ahead along a right field edge and when the hedge ends follow a line of electric poles across an open field to Church Lane and turn left.

3 At the A143 turn left for just a few yards and cross to a track which is the continuation of Church Lane. Follow this into Church Close and through to the old main road and Redenhall Church. The public footpath is to the right, just beyond the church but within the churchyard, so it can be reached by going through the gateway almost opposite the end of the Close. Redenhall Church, also dedicated to St. Mary, is noted for the magnificent Perpendicular tower; built on a hill, it is visible for miles around. It is the main church for Harleston, Redenhall and Wortwell and the boundary between the civil parishes of Redenhall with Harleston and Wortwell goes right through the middle of the church. Join up with the signed path to go left up the hill, ignoring a path going to the right. At the top of the churchyard go through a gate and continue ahead along a field edge, then turn right along Cook's Lane. When the road bends to the left, go ahead along a narrower lane. When this bends to the right turn left on a footpath. After about 650 yards turn left at a fingerpost then immediately left again, rejoining the Angles Way, this follows the left side of a ditch. Continue to a road and turn right for a short distance, turn left onto a cross field path just before a road sign for crossroads ahead. Go diagonally across the field towards a stile which is a little to the right of a field gate. *(As an alternative, if the field is very wet, stay on the road, turning left at the crossroads.)*

At the end of the footpath turn left and either follow the road back into Mendham directly to the starting point, or take a short diversion around All Saints Church.

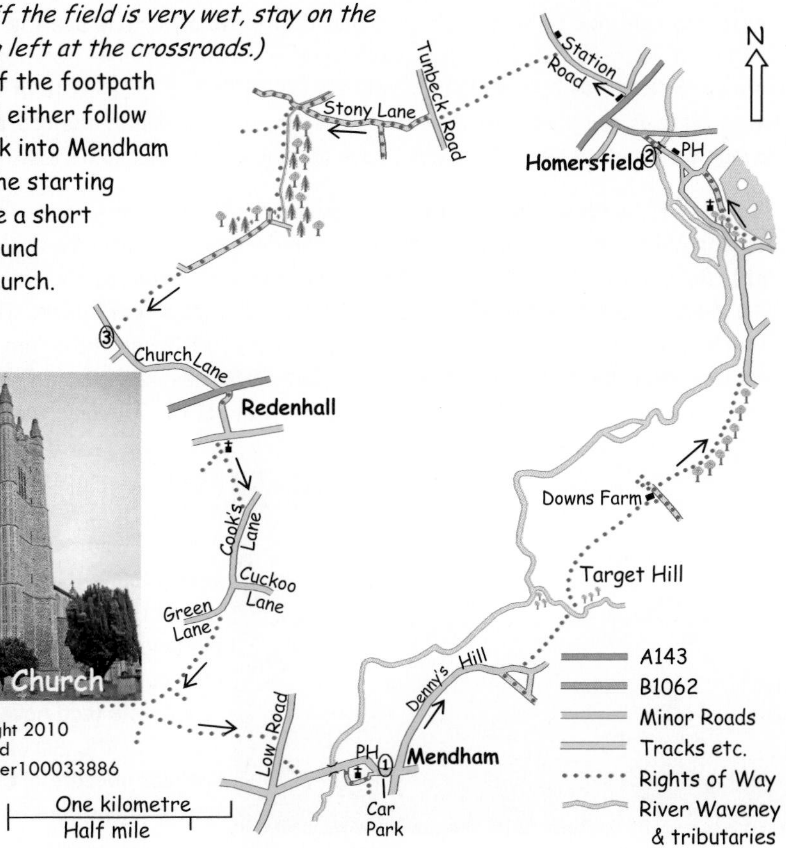

Redenhall Church

© Crown copyright 2010
All rights reserved
OS Licence number100033886

One kilometre
Half mile

N

Tunbeck Road

Station Road

Stony Lane

Homersfield

PH

Church Lane

Redenhall

Cook's Lane

Cuckoo Lane

Green Lane

Downs Farm

Target Hill

Denny's Hill

Low Road

PH

Mendham

Car Park

━━━	A143
━━━	B1062
━━━	Minor Roads
━━━	Tracks etc.
·····	Rights of Way
～～	River Waveney & tributaries

24 West Acre and Castle Acre – Seven miles.
OS - L 132, E 236, Ref 787150.

This walk starts from West Acre, at a parking place half a mile east of the village. The route uses part of the Nar Valley Way, the 34 mile route between King's Lynn and Gressenhall. Although our circuit just skims the edge of Castle Acre, you may wish to adapt it to include a visit to the priory and the castle, or you may be seeking refreshments (there are public houses and cafes).

Ford at South Acre

Alternatively you may prefer to start from Castle Acre. In any event the map provides sufficient detail to enable you to choose. The Stewardship agreement for the path and the open access field used in section 2 ends in September 2012, but access may continue to be available beyond that date; otherwise use the road past the church. See walk 18 for a walk eastwards from Castle Acre. For those who would like a much longer walk it could be combined with this one for a route of around twelve milea or more, possibly reversing the direction of one of the routes. See the OS map for a link between Fincham Drove (this walk) and Ruckold's Lane (walk 18).

The ruins of the Cluniac priory and the Norman castle are in the care of English Heritage (there is a charge for entrance to the priory, but entry to the castle is free). Both are well worth a visit. The impressive west front of the priory gives some indication of how the whole must have looked when it was intact. The castle motte and bailey is one of the finest in the country. Although the original stone structure, built by William de Warenne 1st Earl of Surrey, was planned as a country house not a fortification, it was transformed around 1140. The priory was founded by the 2nd Earl, also William. The town was walled and the Bailey Gate still survives.

Castle Acre Priory

The large impressive church, dedicated to St. James, is mainly Perpendicular - usually you will find it open. The town, little larger than a village, has many buildings of architectural interest. Readers who are new to Norfolk (and have not already visited Castle Acre) should perhaps allocate one day for the town and another for the walk.

1 From the parking area face back towards the road to turn left along a track signed "Ford" and "Unsuitable for motors". After a few yards turn right on a crossing path, cross a footbridge and continue along the path, part of the Nar Valley Way. Eventually the path joins Fulmer Lane where you bear right, continuing as it becomes Common Road. Follow this as it bends sharply left.

2 Immediately beyond the bend turn right on a crossing Conservation footpath, a fenced off route along the field edge, and continue until the wall around Castle Acre Priory is immediately ahead. Turn right into a Conservation open access field and go ahead on a path. When this divides, take the right hand route closer to the river, go between a wall and a fence and turn right onto a road, joining the Peddars Way to go over the footbridge beside a ford.

3 Continue along the Peddars Way, going ahead over the cross roads, until, a few yards short of the main road, you turn very sharply right along Fincham Drove. At crossing tracks go straight ahead following a public bridleway sign. Continue on this track, crossing Petticoat Drove and Washpit Drove. Pass a small triangular wood, Three-cocked-hat Plantation, and one more field on your right, then turn onto the track on the right. Go ahead to a road, cross and continue ahead along a footpath, turn right on a track and follow the Nar Valley Way back to the car park.

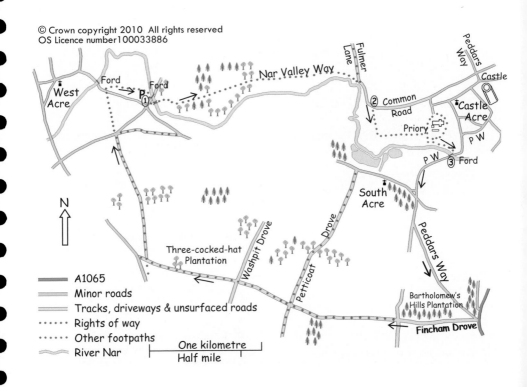

25 Redgrave and Lopham Fen - Seven and a quarter miles.
OS - L 144, E 230, Ref 053803

This walk starts from the Redgrave and Lopham Fen Visitor Centre on the Norfolk/ Suffolk borders (Lopham in Norfolk and Redgrave in Suffolk). This national nature reserve, of international importance, is in the care of the Suffolk Wildlife Trust and is noted for the rare Great Raft Spider, but you are much more likely to meet the hardy Konik Polski, which were bred in Poland to recreate the extinct Tarpan horses. They are allowed to roam around the Fen, and their grazing helps to maintain the open landscape and prevents invasive scrub taking hold. They were chosen because they are able to tolerate the wet conditions of the Fen far better than any British breed. The Visitor Centre is generally open at weekends and some weekdays during most school holidays; the Fen is open daily and the car park is available for visitors. This walk, on both sides of the county boundary, visits Blo' Norton Fen, a small part of Thelnetham Fen and also Hinderclay Fen. The Suffolk part of the walk is almost entirely along the Angles Way, the long distance walkers' route between Knettishall Heath and Great Yarmouth. For information about Redgrave and Lopham Fen visit www.suffolkwildlife.co.uk and for the other Fens www.lohp.org.uk. Unfortunately there is not sufficient space here for much detail, but it is well worth finding out more. It is said that the B1113 over the county boundary, between the sources of the two rivers, is the only place where it is possible to properly enter Norfolk without crossing water. The boundary mostly follows the rivers although it does wander away in places, especially to the west, and some parts of both counties are on the "wrong" side.

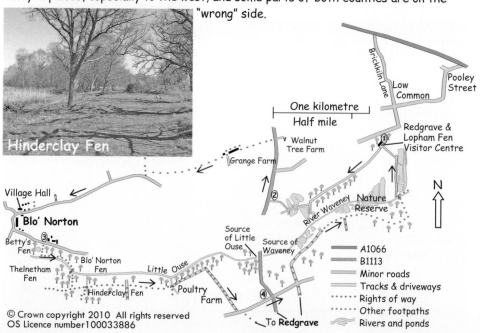

© Crown copyright 2010 All rights reserved
OS Licence number 100033886

1 From the car park go through the gate to the left of the Visitor Centre, ignore a gate to the left and go through the gate straight ahead. Carry on along the track, keeping ahead through more gates. Eventually the track enters woodland and shortly swings to the left. A few yards beyond this point turn right along the Waveney Trail. Continue across the first crossing track (signed "no entry" on both sides) then at the next crossway the Waveney Trail goes left, but our way turns right, by a yellow marker, towards large and small gates to exit into a track leading to the B1113. To the south, on either side of the road between our outward and return routes, are the sources of the River Waveney and the Little Ouse. The two rivers, rising within a few yards of one another, flow in entirely different directions; the Waveney flows east and the Little Ouse goes west to flow eventually into the Great Ouse.

2 Turn right along the road, pass a junction on the right and continue to a drive-way leading to Walnut Tree Farm. Turn left along a footpath opposite, following the line of electric poles. At the agricultural buildings, still shown as Grange Farm on O.S. maps, follow the waymarks round to your right and then back on to the original line of the path. The route is then waymarked along a field edge from the top end of an access track. Keep ahead through a field boundary and over a foot-bridge, to the next boundary, pass through and turn left onto a track and very shortly right along a quiet minor road. Ignore a turning on the right and continue to Blo' Norton, pass a red telephone box and the village hall, then turn left. Turn left again – signposted to South Lopham, Redgrave and via The Banks.

3 Pass the sign for the end of the 30 limit and on reaching the next group of houses on the left, immediately before the gate of the first one, turn right into Betty's Fen, which is adjacent to Blo' Norton Fen. At a T junction turn left along the river bank and continue to the bridge over the Little Ouse. This bridge was officially opened in April 2006, creating options for a greater variety of walks. Cross the bridge and turn left to follow the winding path which joins the Angles Way, turn left again across an open field to a footbridge into Hinderclay Fen. Follow the path, going straight over a crossing track, eventually bearing left through trees to cross a bridge, follow the track behind a poultry farm turning right at a corner and out to a road, turn left and continue ahead.

4 Go straight on across B1113 and then shortly after the de-restriction sign turn left at the crossing tracks. Go through a gate and bear right with the track. Shortly after passing a water works ignore a path to the left and go ahead through a gate. Continue along the path, pass a public footpath to the right and continue along the woodland path which eventually bears to the left and leads to a bridge over the Waveney. (This last section of path can be rather muddy) Cross and turn left then almost immediately right onto a broad track leading back to the Visitor Centre.

26 Great Ellingham – Seven and a half miles.
OS - L 144, E 237, Ref 022970

This walk starts just on the south eastern edge of the village of Great Ellingham, almost precisely two miles from the centre of Attleborough. A fair proportion of the walk follows tracks, good for winter walking, however some field paths are included. At the time of writing they were clearly marked, but at times they may be ploughed, awaiting reinstatement. This does not affect your right to walk on them, although it may make it a little harder to follow the route. Park on the lay-by, on the right hand side of the B1077 from Attleborough, just before 30 limit sign.

1 Cross the road, turn right along the verge, and turn left on a path immediately before bungalows. It leads through the car park of the Crown PH. Turn right along the road to the Church. St. James, a large church, dates from the early 14th century, and has some beautiful chequered flushwork with knapped flint and stone blocks. Continue to the main road and go straight across into Deopham Road. After just over 500 yards turn left over a footbridge and along a field edge footpath with large hedge. When the field edge bends to the left, go right over a footbridge and follow a narrow path along the inside edge of a wooded area. Keep to the left past commercial premises and out to a road via a gap in the corner. Turn left along the verge, then almost immediately right along a lane signposted "Bow Street". After about 500 yards and just after a left bend in the road, turn right along a signed path across a field and at the far side go over the ditch and turn right along the field edge. After about a hundred yards the path turns left across the field towards the middle of the group of the three poultry sheds. Just behind the sheds the path goes over a culvert and (at the time of writing) through a very small gap between straw bales, obviously subject to change. Bear slightly left to go between the second and third sheds (from the right) and out to Wood Lane. Turn right, then soon left along a grassy track. From this point onwards, until the edge of Goose Common, nearly a mile and a half away, there are unofficial realignments of the rights of way. Both the definitive and alternative paths are shown on the sketch map, but the permissive routes are described here as they provide easier walking. However unofficial diversions such as these do make it much more difficult to plan a walk in the country-

side. Continue along the track, go through a field boundary, and turn right to follow the field edge to a track ahead marked "Private". Turn left, then turn right after 100 yards for Little Ellingham. Turn left to St. Peter's Church – the tower is 13th or early 14th century, but most of the rest of the church was rebuilt after a disastrous fire in 1867 (the key is available at number 5 opposite).

Looking back to Gt. Ellingham

2 Turn left on a signed footpath adjacent to Church Avenue from the bend in the road. When the path reaches open fields it bends slightly right then to the left to go straight across a field, then continues along a field edge. At a corner where the green track goes round to the left, go ahead a little to the right diagonally across the open field towards a wooded corner. Go over a footbridge to Goose Common and take the path going ahead, join a track out to a road and turn right on the road alongside the Common. At a junction go straight across to a broad track. When the track ahead goes into a garden turn left, following the track alongside a wood. Soon, where a short track goes off to the right into the wood you may choose to carry straight on or take a permissive woodland route, but in any event it is worth taking a small detour for a view of Rockland Mere. Turn along the woodland track and the mere is soon visible on the left. From this point you may return to the main track or take a permissive path on the right, it goes over a footbridge and winds through the wood before rejoining the main track at the other end of the wood via the car park for the fishing lakes. Both routes are very attractive and it may be worth while making a complete circuit and then retracing your steps along the main track. Whichever option you follow continue along the access track for the lakes to a road on a corner.

Little Ellingham

Lay's Farm

Goose Common

Rockland Mere

Wood Lane

Bow Street

	B1077
	Minor roads
	Tracks & driveways
......	Rights of way
......	Other footpaths

N

Rockland St. Peter

Rockland All Saints

Great Ellingham

Deopham Road

Mill Lane

PH

Mill Lane

One kilometre

Half mile

3 Go ahead through Rockland St. Peter, cross the main road and continue ahead. After about 200 yards you may turn right along a track to visit St. Peter's Church, which is open every day. In 1948 it suffered a fire which destroyed the thatched roof and much of the interior, but it was sympathetically restored and is quite delightful. Return to the road, turn right, continue ahead to a junction and turn left along Mill Lane. When the road turns sharply right, continue ahead on the track all the way back to Great Ellingham. Turn right, then almost immediately left along Rectory Lane, keep round to the right, turn left at the T junction then back through the car park of the Crown and along the footpath used at the start of the walk.

27 Loddon Ingloss - Seven and a half miles.
OS - L 134, E OL40, Ref 345955

This walk starts in Loddon Ingloss, the south western tail of the parish of Loddon. Ingloss was mentioned in the Domesday Book: it had 3 villans, 7 bordars and 9 soke

Water Tower

men, there were 4 pigs and one horse. It is still not densely inhabited, the OS map just shows the Manor House, Manor Farm, two pairs of semi-detached Manor Farm Cottages plus Bush Farm to the east just off our map. It also has a water tower where the walk starts and there is space to park on the verge.

The route described at the beginning of section 2 is a permissive alternative to the definitive right of way, agreed by the landowner and Norfolk County Council. Both routes are shown on the map, but unofficial diversions do cause difficulties for walkers trying to follow a route on an OS map.

1 Start along the very narrow path on the left of the water tower between the fence and the hedge. Continue along the hedge, following it to the left and right and into a narrow green lane. Follow this round to the left, then turn right along a broader track for about 100 yards to a road. Thwaite St. Mary Church is on the left. It has a richly carved Norman doorway, the tower is 15th century and the chancel dates from 1738, but was altered in 1861. Return to the route and continue ahead along a footpath. Go through a gate and across a pony field to a stile, follow the field edge then turn right along a broad track. Continue ahead when the track meets a surfaced track on a bend – this would once have been a through road but was cut by a wartime airfield to the west, so there is now unlikely to be much traffic. Continue ahead at a crossroads to the next junction and turn left along a footpath, starting as a track, then becoming a field edge path. Continue ahead ignoring a footpath to the right, but at a waymark and a crossing path take the right fork. Follow the field edge then go over two stiles and out to a road. Turn left to St. Peter's Mundham, which also has an elaborate Norman doorway – were Thwaite

Sisland St. Mary

and Mundham keeping up with the Norman equivalent of the Joneses? The tower is Perpendicular. Mundham had two parish churches until 1749 and small remains of St Ethelbert's are half a mile away to the east near Abbey Farm. Go up the steps into the churchyard and exit down the steps at the other end back to the road, then immediately turn right on a footpath.

2 From the rear corner of the churchyard follow the permissive diagonal path going half right across the field. Turn left alongside the hedge on the opposite side and continue to a field corner; the path goes through slightly to the right, then through a garden, skirting around Springhill, to join a driveway. Now turn right at a T junction, then right where it joins a road on a corner. Just beyond a post box on the right go left along a track. Turn right at the next road, then left onto a footpath. Follow the field-edge path until it reaches a corner, the waymarked route then goes a little to the left diagonally across the open field, where another waymark is visible on the opposite side. The path then follows a hedge again for a short distance, before going right, through the hedge and ahead across another field. Continue along a track to a road and turn right to St. Mary's Church Sisland. This little church, with newly thatched roof and wooden bell cote, the walls newly whitewashed, could have come straight out of a picture book. It's much older predecessor was destroyed by lightning at three o'clock on the afternoon of 12th July 1761 during Sunday service. It was soon rebuilt, but the new building is much smaller than the old, just replacing the south aisle, which explains why it is so very long and narrow.

3 Continue along the road, turn right at a junction then right again on the Mundham Road. Turn left onto a footpath on a bend opposite a house, ignore the diagonal path to the right and bear round to the left to follow the field edge. At the first crossing boundary the path joins a track on a Corner. At the next field corner the track goes round to the left, but the footpath continues straight ahead. On reaching a wooded pit go briefly left then right at a sign going round to the east. Fork left just beyond the pit and follow the path across the field. At the far side cross a track, go over a stile and through a paddock and out to the road. Turn right along the road and back to the water tower.

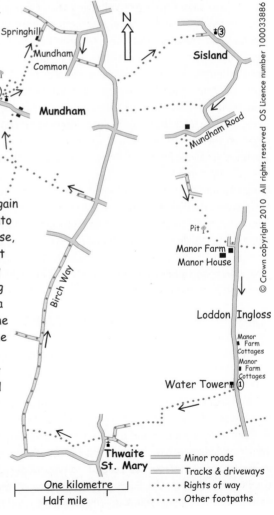

Minor roads
Tracks & driveways
Rights of way
Other footpaths

One kilometre
Half mile

28 Holt Country Park and Baconsthorpe Castle -
Eight and a half miles.   OS - L 133, E 251 & 252, Ref 082376

Holt Country Park is only a short distance south of Holt. It has several waymarked trails and on its own is well worth a visit. An attractive informative leaflet is available free, direct from Norfolk County Council (phone 01603 222769) or for a small charge from tourist information centres etc. This walk could easily be divided into two, both via Hempstead, the eastern segment starting from Baconsthorpe Castle - also well worth a visit, even without the walk. Park on the main car park, access from the B1149, where there is a Visitor Centre and toilets.

1 Start by going through a gap beside the information board on the right. Turn left and soon fork right following the "Circular Walks" sign. When the path gets close to the road and a CW sign indicates right, turn left to a pond, bear round to the left and fork right at the next junction along a broad straight path. Go through a gate and cross a track, continue ahead and at the next T junction turn right, then bend round to the left with the path, cross another track with a metal gate on your right, continue ahead, turn right and out to Hempstead Road. After almost half a mile, turn right on a signed track along a field edge. At a junction of fields bear a little to the right then to the left, keeping to field edges on the left. Go through a gap on the left at a field corner, follow the path past a pond, over a stile and continue towards farm buildings. Follow a track to the left then to the right, passing the entrance of Hempstead Hall. Keep to the driveway, ignoring a path on the left. Opposite a bungalow with a long leylandii hedge, turn right over a footbridge to a field path. As it approaches trees cross a ditch to the right, continue ahead for a short distance, bear round to the right along the field edge, then bend left to All Saints Church Hempstead. This delightful little church has its origins in the 11th century and every century up to the 20th has made some alteration or addition. The tower, no taller than the rest of the church, is just attached by one corner. Continue (either inside or outside the churchyard) to a road and turn left.

2 As the road curves to the left, and just beyond a terrace of very attractive cottages, turn right through a gap beside a field gate. Continue to a road, cross into a field and turn right along the field edge adjacent to the road. At a crossing field boundary turn left along the field edge, continue to a corner, and go through a gap. Turn right along a hedged path, then follow a field edge to Beckett's Farm, cross a track and continue ahead along a lane. Turn left along Hall Lane to Hall Farm and Baconsthorpe Castle. Turn right, then left through the car park into the Castle. A moat on three sides and a mere on the eastern side make an idyllic setting for this fortified manor house, built in the 15th century by the Heydon family. Within 200 years financial difficulties forced its partial demolition and sale of the stone for building materials. The ruins are in the care of English Heritage and it is open at all reasonable times and there are informative display panels outlining the history.

3 Emerging from the Castle, turn left out of the car park along the access track. Just before a bend and a cattle grid, turn right over a footbridge, then go ahead bearing a little to the left. In a corner go over a footbridge and continue following field edges to the right and left and out to a road in Baconsthorpe. Turn briefly right, then left along a minor road and turn right at a junction by a water tower. Continue for just over half a mile, ignoring a road junction on the right and crossing footpaths to a junction with a track marked as a private road and two rights of way. Turn half right across an open field. At the time of writing this was clearly visible, but sometimes it could be awaiting reinstatement after ploughing or cultivation, in which case it is worth remembering that it runs roughly at a right angle to the private road. Part way across the field a dip in the landscape ahead with a road running through it becomes apparent; the footpath goes just to the right of the dip. Go through a gap down steps (backwards with care) into Back Lane.

4 Turn left then right along the road. Continue to a junction and go straight across to a footpath. Beyond a short section along a track the path goes ahead across an open field. A gap is visible ahead, go through and over a stile, turn right and soon left to follow field edges. At a large square barn turn left and right to follow Mill House Lane. Turn left at the bottom of a hill, keep to the main path crossing the River Glaven by a culvert. At the top of the hill keep ahead and as the path meets the road bear a little to the right to keep more or less parallel with the road. At junctions, when in doubt go to the left in order to keep close to the road. On re-entering the Country Park the route is straight, wider and very clear and eventually meets the entrance to the car park.

Hempstead Church

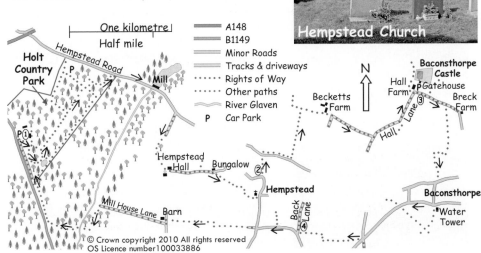

▬▬	A148
▬▬	B1149
▬▬	Minor Roads
▬▬	Tracks & driveways
⋯⋯	Rights of Way
⋯⋯	Other paths
∿∿	River Glaven
P	Car Park

One kilometre
Half mile

Holt Country Park
Hempstead Road
Mill
Beccketts Farm
Baconsthorpe Castle
Hall Farm
Gatehouse
Breck Farm
Hall Lane
N
Hempstead Hall
Bungalow
Hempstead
Mill House Lane
Barn
Back Lane
Baconsthorpe
Water Tower

29 Emily's Wood, Weeting – Nine & a half miles, shorter option 6 miles.
OS - L 144+143, E 229, Ref 798895 (or 777891 for shorter option)

This walk starts from the parking area by Emily's Wood along the western side of the A1065. The narrow, but long (almost a mile) parking area is marked on the OS maps. A rough track runs along the whole length with three or four access links from the road; parking about half way along is suggested. For the shorter option park near Weeting Castle and St Mary's Church and walk northwards, via Home Farm. Join the main route at the junction near the old barn half way through section one. It is an easy walk for all seasons, mostly on firm tracks. In summer the wild flowers are delightful, but even in midwinter, as the sandy Breckland soil is well drained, it is unlikely to be very muddy and winter walking offers its own joys. The forest is not all conifers, there are large areas where deciduous trees are more dominant and both contrast with the re-created Hockwold Heath. Throughout Thetford Forest there are several areas that have been returned to heath. The whole area is rich in antiquities, there are several tumuli in the vicinity, mostly hidden in the forest, and the Neolithic flint mines at Grimes Graves are not far away. Weeting Castle, now a ruin in the care of English Heritage, was actually a grand 12th century manor house and was never fortified.

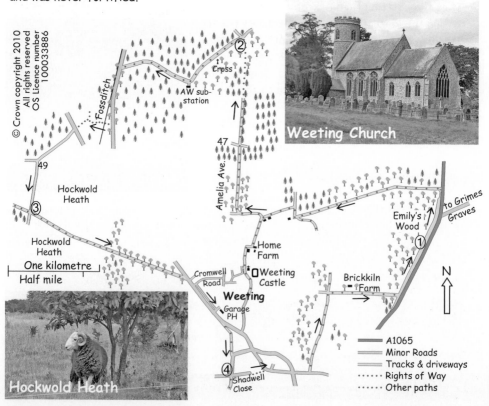

1 Walk northwards along the track with the main road to the right, passing the road to Grimes Graves on the right. When track ceases, continue for a short distance along the verge then go left on a track. At a driveway to a cottage go to the right, then, after about 100 yards, left at a junction. Pass a house and an old barn then fork right *(the shorter walk joins here from the left)* and follow the track as it curves left. At Hall Covert, just before more woodland, turn right along Amelia Avenue. Go across track 47 and continue ahead between a belt of Scots Pine on the right and a field on the left. Keep to the narrowing path through woodland.

2 Go left at crossing tracks. After a quarter of a mile an information board marks a narrow path to the left leading the short way to the remains of a medieval wayside cross, probably dating from the 14th century. It was on a pilgrims' route, across a bare heath, to Walsingham. After visiting the cross return to the main track, keeping right when it passes an Anglia Water sub station on the left. At a road turn left for about two fifths of a mile. Just beyond a slight rise and fall in road turn right along a forest path and cross Fossditch, an ancient earthwork. The remains here are not very spectacular, but the straight line through the landscape is easily identifiable. Fossditch might have been built by Britons trying to keep the Anglo Saxons out, or by the Anglo Saxons as a boundary – or you might prefer the explanation that it was created by the Devil dragging his heel along the ground - and when he knocked the earth off his heel, it formed the mound of Thetford Castle! The boundary between District Councils now follows this part of the ditch. Keep left when the path forks, then go straight across a road onto a wide gravel track, with forest on the right and heath to the left, for about a third of a mile. Now go left at a fork keeping to track number 49 and continue for a further third of a mile.

3 Turn left again onto a crossing byway across Hockwold Heath. Beyond the heath the track passes through a small area of woodland and is then bordered by trees. Turn right along road, cross to a path along the verge, and soon turn left into Cromwell Road. *(For the shorter walk follow this to a T junction, turn right, then left into Edmund Road, first left, first right, left again then down some steps on the right back to the Church.)* For the longer walk turn immediately right along Pilgrims Way, parallel with the busy road, but out of the traffic. At end of Pilgrims Way walk across the grass in front of a garage, then cross the road to a pavement. When the road bears left go straight ahead, then bear right on a footpath and cut-off road with houses to the left. When it rejoins the road (Hockwold Road) cross and continue along the pavement to a junction.

4 Turn left along Shadwell Close, almost to the end, then bear right on to a foot- path. At its end go ahead then bear right with houses left and a field on the right. Cross Brandon Road and go ahead along a road signposted Mundford. After about 200 yards turn left along a track towards trees. Continue for about half a mile, then turn right across a field towards Brickkiln Farm (amongst trees), keep ahead along the track back to the A1065 and then left along the car park.

30 Wells-next-the-Sea – Ten miles, shorter option seven & a half miles.
OS - L 132, E 251. Ref 918432.

This walk starts from St. Nicholas Church in Church Plain, Wells-next-the-Sea. The name was derived from the numerous fresh water springs and wells in the area and "next-the-Sea" was added in the early 19th century to distinguish it from other places with the same name, although Wells-on-Sea was also used at times. However it is neither quite on or next to the sea, being about a mile inland from open water, but it does have a sheltered harbour and was a port for over 700 years. Now it is just used by fishing and pleasure boats. The town is well worth exploring with many listed buildings in its narrow streets and alleyways. St. Nicholas Church is Perpendicular, but is largely a reconstruction after it was struck by lightning and badly damaged in 1879.

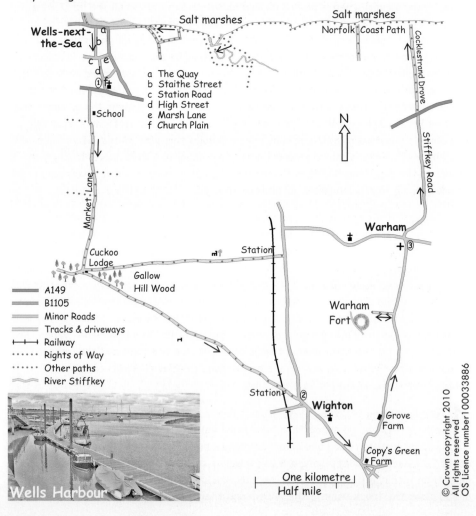

a The Quay
b Staithe Street
c Station Road
d High Street
e Marsh Lane
f Church Plain

A149
B1105
Minor Roads
Tracks & driveways
Railway
Rights of Way
Other paths
River Stiffkey

Wells Harbour

1 Turn right out of Church Plain along the A149, then take the first turning to the left along Market Lane. Soon after passing the High School the road ends and the route continues as a track. Keep ahead for about a mile to Cuckoo Lodge. *For the shorter route, take the first turning on the left and follow the track and roads to Warham;* otherwise bear left along the track following the boundary south of Gallow Hill Wood. After about a mile and a half cross the Wells and Walsingham Light Railway by Wighton Halt station, then join a road on a bend. The railway, on four miles of old Great Eastern track from Wells to Walsingham, is the longest $10\frac{1}{4}$ inch narrow gauge steam railway in the world. The unique Garratt locomotive "Norfolk Hero" was specially built for this line and the train normally runs between late March and October (see www.wellswalsinghamrailway.co.uk, or phone 01328 711630).

2 Continue ahead, then, as the main road bends to the right, go straight ahead through Wighton. All Saints Church on the left is large and imposing; sited on the top of a rise, it is visible for miles around. Much of the church is 15th century. The west tower, over 650 years old, fell during a storm in 1965 (fortunately away from the church) but amazingly was rebuilt ten years later due to a Canadian benefactor, Leeds Richardson, as a memorial to some of his ancestors who came from the village. Keep along the road beyond the village and turn sharp left just before Copy's Green Farm. Keep along the lane for about a mile, then turn left along a track for Warham Camp. The Camp by the River Stiffkey is a late Iron Age hill fort, maybe dating from around 50 BC. It had double banks and ditches and an inner rampart, much damaged by 18th century landscaping and the straightening of the river. Excavations in 1959 revealed evidence of buildings and rubbish from the first century AD, indicating Romano-British occupation. There are wide views from the top of the banks. Return to the lane and turn left towards Warham village. Before the cross roads, All Saints Church is on the left; it is beautifully situated on a hill just outside the village. It was once much larger; the base of the tower remains, but the aisles have gone except two bays remaining as transepts. Two of the three fonts are Norman, the chancel is early 14th century, but there was much Victorian restoration. Warham has another church, St Mary Magdalen, half a mile to the west along the Holt Road, on the shorter route.

3 Go ahead over the cross roads in the village centre *(the shorter route rejoins the main route here)*. After about a mile cross the A149 to go along Cocklestrand Drove to the coastal path, part of The Peddars Way and Norfolk Coast Path National Trail. Turn left and follow the path along the edge of the salt marshes all the way back into Wells. This western end of seven miles of salt marsh between Wells and Blakeney, one of the most extensive in Northern Europe, is part of the Holkham Nature Reserve. Venturing onto the marsh can be dangerous and could damage plants or disturb the birds. It is a haven for a host of wading birds and wildfowl. Plants such as sea lavender, able to survive flooding and salt, thrive without competition from plants with more usual needs. In Wells continue along The Quay, go left into Staithe Street, cross Station Road and follow the High Street back to Church Plain.

Location of Walks

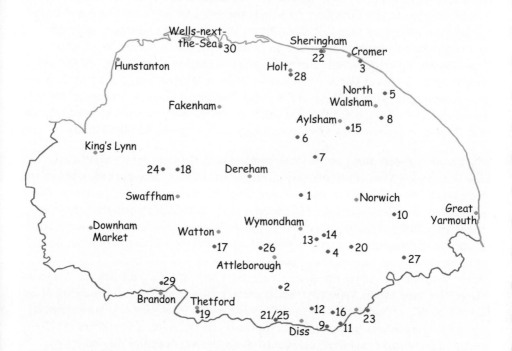

The green numbered dots indicate the approximate location
of the starting points of each of the 30 walks

Countryside Code

Be safe, plan ahead and follow any signs.

Leave gates and property as you find them.

Protect plants and animals and take your litter home.

Keep dogs under close control.

Consider other people.